Penny Dis

By Robert Jackson

WTL INTERNATIONAL

PENNY DIS

Copyright © 2024 Robert Jackson
WTL International has obtained
sole publishing rights.

All rights reserved. No part of this publication may be reproduced in any form or by any electronic or mechanical means, including information storage and material systems, except in the case of brief quotations embodied in critical articles or reviews, without permission in writing from its publisher, WTL International.

Published by
WTL International
930 North Park Drive
P.O. Box 33049
Brampton, Ontario
L6S 6A7 Canada
www.wtlipublishing.com

978-1-778310-34-8

Penny Dis

(Think seriously about this)

*40 thought-provoking,
Bible-based meditations
to revitalize your Christian walk*

Robert Jackson

ENDORSEMENTS

Michael Miller

Penny Dis is a rich collection of biblically based impactful vignettes compiled in a unique and creative style. They each convey age-old gospel truths in a manner that is easy to identify with. Robert Jackson teaches through real-life applications by inserting himself in the stories to make theology "walk in human shoes." By doing this, he appeals to the common person who desires to 'lead a quiet and peaceable life in all godliness and reverence' (1Timothy 2:2).

Robert places the "cookies" where they can be reached by all as he shares gems and truths from the Word of God. The messages are clear, simple, and easy to grasp and apply. Keeping it simple, yet profound, Robert manages to present deep spiritual truths in an uncomplicated way which points ultimately to his Lord and Saviour Jesus Christ, who is the Way the Truth and the Life for all of us who need a saviour from sin and its penalty.

Readers, ranging across the spectrum, from the "churched" to the "unchurched" will find this book touches on areas of common concern and provides insights into how to approach them. If you would like to read a book that presents theological and biblical truths in an unconventional manner, yet without compromising biblical fidelity, I present to you *Penny Dis*.

~Michael Miller
Former student of Robert Jackson
and very good friend

Veronica Green

When you talk about a man with a voice, Robert comes to mind. His is a voice that comes with two meanings: the deep strong voice that you recognize from a distance, the voice you could pick out on school grounds, coming from a classroom or from an auditorium where a PTA Meeting is being held. It is the voice of a teacher on duty, doing his job.

Then, there is this same voice you hear as you read any of the devotions Robert has penned. This voice now takes on a new tone as you hear the conviction, the dedication, and the commitment of a Christian expressing and teaching God's Word with the power to convince and convict the reader.

Robert's writings are uplifting and what makes it impacting is the fact that the writings are drawn from personal experiences. I have received plenty from reading Robert's messages. Many have opened my eyes to different perspectives on a well-known, or not so well-known, Bible verse or passage.

Overall, now that Robert's writings are all in his book *Penny Dis*, it makes re-

reading easily accessible, just in case you want to hear that particular message again.

~Veronica Green
Author, Life and Laughter
on the Other Man's Grass, 2013

Claudette Mignott

It has been quite some time now that I have had the privilege of reading *Penny Dis*, which our dear brother would send to me, sometimes three times per week, especially during the lockdown of the world as a result of COVID 19.

Robert's writings are so practical, down to earth, God-centered, and thought provoking. They always give me a glimmer of hope, especially when I am facing challenging times.

There were times Robert's writings would reveal his early childhood, which was full of anecdotes, but at the end of each writing, one leaves wanting to dig deeper into the Word of God.

I always look forward to the words of precious hymns Robert includes, ones which we no longer sing at church services. It is like walking down memory lane.

I am happy that the writings of my brother are now compiled in a devotional form for many others to read and be blessed... and also to grow more in the love of God.

~Claudette Mignott
Longstanding Christian friend

Stephen and Ranti Olasina

"A town built on a hill cannot be hidden. Neither do people light a lamp and put it under a bowl" (Saint Matthew 5:14–15, NIV). Our dear brother Robert is using his deep mix of childhood, adult life and faith experiences to bring powerful, yet soothing messages of reflection and refreshment to our personal engagement with the Almighty God. We are both delighted to endorse *Penny Dis* as a down-to-earth exposition of God's truths in the life of an active, born-again Christian encouraging us to seek Him regularly.

~Stephen and Ranti Olasina
Robert's small group leaders

Malcolm John Frazer

If you are one of those persons wishing you have a "Life's Tour Guidebook," then your wish has arrived! Bobby, as we affectionately call Robert Jackson, has carefully mixed together Christian theology and the need to order our steps aright.

Bobby invites you to think about a subject and before you know it, your feet are already engaged and taking you in the right direction. *Penny Dis* is packed with multiple invitations to step up to a higher level. And as you notice a change in altitude, you begin to realize that this journey is not a plateau!

It is without any reservations that I wholeheartedly recommend *Penny Dis* for your personal spiritual Guidebook! Your spirit, soul and body will thank you.

~Malcolm John Frazer
Mentor and family friend

Aisha Hammah

I am happy for the opportunity to publish *Penny Dis*. Begin to read it and you will see that author Robert Jackson was uniquely created for this work. The text is steeped in Scripture, aptly chosen. Robert also exercises his skill for narration as he narrates events of the Bible in touching and amusing ways. He employs a great deal of insight, reading in between the lines of The Bible to draw out possible aspects of the stories you never even knew could be there to enliven the reading experience. All the while, it is Biblically sound.

Everyday applications of Scripture and Biblical principles are intelligently used to teach core truths and to let us evaluate our lives. You will read and read over this material to plant the seeds, nourish the seeds, and draw a great harvest from the seeds of a steadfast belief in the precious God of the Bible, which are embedded in *Penny Dis*. It will convict you, but it will cleanse you. It is a living work.

~Aisha Hammah
Publisher, WTL International

Pastor Chris Shipley

Over the past few years, I have had the privilege of receiving regular devotional thoughts from my brother, Robert Jackson. Early in the morning, I would receive a text sharing an insightful story that highlighted a biblical truth or a call to Christ-like transformation in light of the gospel. I was pleased to hear that these daily devotionals had been collected into a volume that you now hold in your hand to enjoy morning or evening. I pray that they will be as much of a blessing to you as they have been to me. May the Lord bless many through this volume as they seek Christ fully!

~Pastor Chris Shipley
Pastor of Soul Care and Global Sending,
Hope Church, Mississauga

ACKNOWLEDGEMENTS

Ten lepers were cleansed by Jesus one day, and only one (a Samaritan) returned to give thanks. I hasten to follow the example of the grateful tithe.

I have so much to give thanks for. I thank God for saving this lost sinner and adopting me into His glorious family. I thank Him for the Spirit's insight into His precious word and the unique way He enables me to communicate it to others. Penny Dis is dedicated to Your glory, Jesus.

My heart is full of gratitude for the love of my life, Sandra Marie. You have loved me, prayed for me, rebuked me (when necessary), but never left my side. I love you dearly and thank you for helping to give meaning and purpose to my life. What would I ever do without you? Thanks also for meticulously typing the original manuscript.

Aisha, my publisher, what can I say? Tears have given way to great joy. You know what I mean. At times, you were even more excited about *Penny Dis* than I was. Thank you for your smile, mild manner, and professional efficiency. The Lord bless you in your future endeavours.

To my friends who have endorsed this book, I am so grateful that you have supported this dream. My heart is overwhelmed.

Finally, I thank my family (natural and spiritual) for your encouragement over these years. I took your advice. *Penny Dis* is put in print. Thanks for believing in me.

I give *Penny Dis* to the world. Read and be blessed. Obey and be fulfilled.

~Robert (Bobby) Jackson

TABLE OF CONTENTS

He Leadeth Me …1
Stay Connected …7
Finishing Strong …13
Apathy, Sympathy, and Empathy …19
Who Sinned? …25
The Blessedness of Brokenness …31
Even If You Don't …37
Scars in Heaven …43
Lift Your Head Up High, Your
　　　Redemption Draws Nigh …47
Look Up! …51
Childish or Childlike? …55
The Gift of the Present …61
Man on the Middle Cross …67
Fully Known, Fully Loved …73
Past Your Past …81
Wounded Soldier, Battle On …87
God's Not Done with You …93
Truth Be Told …99
Out of My Hands, Into Yours …107
When God Says "Time's Up" …113

TABLE OF CONTENTS

CONTINUED

God of the Hills and Valleys ...119
Pride Aside ...125
The Pursuit of Happiness ...133
Good Looks ...139
But for the Grace of God ...147
Oh Freedom! ...153
Life Unlimited ...161
Promises, Promises ...169
Holy Forever ...175
Be Real ...181
The Potter's Hand ...187
That's the Thing About Praise ...191
What Have You Got in Your Hand? ...195
Made for More ...201
Not in Closets ...207
What's in a Name? ...217
The Ultimate Transformation ...223
The Power of One ...229
Too Busy Dong What? ...233
What (or Whom) Are You Willing to Die For? ...239

1

HE LEADETH ME

I fondly remember when, many years ago, a childhood friend, who later became my best man, led the youth group on a hike to the Blue Mountains in Jamaica. We went by bus late that evening to Whitfield Hall (an inn of sorts) where we rested for a few hours before we made the trek up the treacherous trails a few hours before dawn. At the time, I thought it was odd that we had set out in darkness, but I had confidence in our guide who had made the journey on numerous occasions with a hiking group named PTJI (Peak Tours Jamaica Incorporated).

As we journeyed in the pitch blackness, we followed in single file behind Philip, who told us to follow his instructions explicitly and to echo his instructions down the line to those behind. I can still recall the echo: "keep to the left... keep to the left... keep to the left... keep to the left. Then, "keep to the right... keep to the right... keep to the right... keep to the right. We carefully followed on. Then there were the complaints and questions of the weary, "Are we there yet?" To which came the response, "Just around the corner." Now, if you know anything about Jamaican culture, when a Jamaican tells you that where you are going is just around the corner, you have several miles to go. After hearing "just around the corner" more times than they could tolerate, I recall a handful of youths stating that they were not taking another step. They would wait where they sat in exasperation, and so they did, when the peak was indeed just around the next corner. It was so sad that after all that effort, some did not make it to the peak.

Our return journey down the summit was bathed in glorious sunlight. Only then did I understand why our guide had led us to the peak at night. It was now evident why a few hours before, he had told us to keep to the left. To the right were precipices of hundreds of feet. If we had seen this, I am sure many, if not most of us, faint-hearted would have, like the complaining Israelites after the Exodus, wanted to turn back immediately.

Just as our youth guide knew the way so he could lead the way, our Great Shepherd not only knows the way, He is The Way.

It brings to mind the testimony of the psalmist David in the 23rd psalm, "The Lord is my Shepherd." Yes, we silly, vulnerable, follow-fashion, wayward sheep desperately need not only a shepherd, but the Good Shepherd. Because He is that Shepherd, we have no lack. He makes us lie down in green pastures. He leads us beside still waters. He restores our souls. He leads us in paths of righteousness.

Just as our youth guide knew the way so he could lead the way, our Great

Shepherd not only knows the way, He *is* The Way. In the book of Saint John, He says, "I am *the way*, the truth, and the life: no man cometh unto the Father, but by ME" (Saint John 14:6, KJV).

Is He your Shepherd today? Why not lovingly embrace the One who gave His life for the sheep? Then, follow Him.

I am a lover of the great hymns of the past. They are so personal and so powerful. I close this reflection with the words of one such by author Joseph Gilmore.

He Leadeth Me
"He leadeth me, O blessed thought.
O word with heav'nly comfort fraught.
Whate'er I do, where'er I be,
Still 'tis God's hand that leadeth me.

"He leadeth me, He leadeth me.
By His own hand He leadeth me.
His faithful foll'wer I would be.
For by His hand He leadeth me.

"Sometimes 'mid scenes of deepest gloom,
Sometimes where Eden's flowers bloom,

ROBERT JACKSON

By waters still, over troubled sea,
Still 'tis His hand that leadeth me.

"Lord, I would place my hand in Thine,
Nor ever murmur nor repine,
Content, whate'er lot I see,
Since 'tis God's hand that leadeth me.

"And when my task on Earth is done,
When by Thy grace the victory's won,
E'en death's cold wave I will not flee.
Since God through Jordan leadeth me."

Lead me, Lord. I will follow.
PENNY DIS

PENNY DIS

Takeaway(s) / New Idea(s)

_____

_____

_____

_____

_____

Commitment(s)

_____

_____

_____

_____

_____

Prayer / Thanksgiving / Resolution(s)

_____

_____

_____

_____

_____

2

STAY CONNECTED

If you and I remain teachable, some simple everyday experiences can teach some profound spiritual lessons. I was about to mow my lawn this morning and thought everything was in place for the activity. The mower blades were sharp and uncluttered. The extension chord was plugged into the mower. Everything appeared to be ready for action, but when I tried to start the mower, *nothing*... A careful check soon revealed the problem. I had not plugged the extension cord into the power source.

This lawnmower oversight reminds me of Samson, that great man of God ("he man") with a lack of self-control (a "she" problem). Samson had been a miracle child, gifted to a godly couple who had given up on having children. He was the product of a post-menstrual pregnancy. His parents were given instructions as to the rearing of this special child. No razor was to be used upon his head. No drinking of liquor. No contact with dead flesh. The Nazarite vow. As long as Samson was faithful to God, he was endowed with super-human strength that would enable him to deliver Israel from their perennial enemy the Philistines, and this he did... for a time.

Samson had a craving which he refused to put under control. He had raging desire for sexy, ungodly women. Despite his parents' cautions, Samson insisted on fulfilling his desires, which led to his undoing.

He met and "fell in love" with a Philistine woman named Delilah. She was financially contracted to find out the source of his super-human strength, so he could be neutralized and eventually killed. Several times, Delilah tried to coerce Samson into revealing his source of power, and each time, he lied to her. This enabled him to escape the enemy after she revealed to them his lie. He was so blinded (pun intended) that he failed to see he was laying on the lap of a deceiver.

Eventually, Delilah wore Samson down with her beguiling tears, insisting that if he truly loved her, he would tell her the truth. The source of his strength lay in his obedience to God in not cutting the seven locks of his hair. After revealing this to Delilah, Samson fell asleep (again, pun intended) on Delilah's lap, and she had a Philistine soldier cut his locks. Suddenly, Samson was awakened, declaring the Philistine military attack. Samson, not knowing what had been done to him, thought he would do as in previous times and overpower the enemy.

One of the saddest verses in the Bible is Judges 16, verse 20. It says, "He awoke from his sleep and thought, "I will go out as before and shake myself free," but he did not know that the Lord had left him" (Judges 16:20, BSB).

One of the saddest verses in the Bible is Judges 16, verse 20. It says, "He awoke from his sleep and thought, "I will go out as before and shake myself free," but he did not know that the Lord had left him" (Judges 16:20, BSB). Akin to my lawnmower, Samson was not connected to the Power Source, and did not even realize it.

Isn't it also sad that we Christians can continue in sin because there are no immediate consequences (or so it seems) and we believe God will wink at our sin? I am still preaching, and people are still being saved, or teaching my Sunday School class, and students are still enthused, yet sin abounds. Have we forgotten that God is absolutely holy and will not tolerate our hypocritical spiritual games? 'Be not deceived, God is not mocked; as a man (or woman) sows, so shall he also reap' (Galatians 6:7).

My encouragement to you, my readers, and to my own heart, is endeavour to stay connected to God, the Source of our spiritual power.
PENNY DIS

Takeaway(s) / New Idea(s)

_____

_____

_____

_____

_____

Commitment(s)

_____

_____

_____

_____

_____

Prayer / Thanksgiving / Resolution(s)

_____

_____

_____

_____

_____

PENNY DIS

3

FINISHING STRONG

Some dates and occasions are indelibly etched in our minds. For people worldwide, September 11, 2001 is never to be forgotten (for its gravity). For Jamaicans, Hurricane "Wild Gilbert" (September 12, 1988) and August 6, 1962 (when Jamaican Independence was gained) readily come to recollection. Another date can now be added to the collection. The date, August 4, 2024. The place, the Olympics in Paris, France. The event, the men's 100-metre finals.

If you are Jamaican, or a Jamaican sympathizer, your hearts and mine were broken by the feat of one Noah Lyles of the US of A. From the results of the heats and semis, in Jamaican minds, there could only be one outcome for the finals: the gold and silver to Jamaicans Kishane Thompson and Oblique Seville, respectively. Lyles, at best, would be bronze.

I had my apprehensions. Last year at the World Championships, American Sha'Carri Richardson almost did not qualify for the women's 100-metre finals, coming in as one of the third-place finishers, yet she upset the favoured Jamaicans Shericka Jackson and Shelly-Ann Fraser-Pryce. I learned, then, never to count-out "class" American athletes.

American Noah Lyles, like his biblical namesake, gave warning of unlikely but coming disaster, but most Jamaicans, like the people of Noah's day, did not take heed. By the 60-metre mark, it was evident that Seville was out of contention for a medal. Thompson looked good for the gold but was tying up and shortening, and Lyles was making his customary late surge. The rest is history. Lyles... gold by the shortest of margins. Thompson, a disconsolate silver.

There are so many spiritual lessons to be learned. One is that life, not to be compared to a 100-metre dash, can still be embodied by this particular race. The medals are won (or lost) at the 100-metre finish line. You may have the best of starts and executions down the stretch, but many times, it is how you finish that matters.

Return to the Father
and do again the first works of love.

Over the years, I am sure that you have encountered Christians who had amazing stories of conversion. They had wonderful beginnings. They were used by God in powerful ways. However, they fell away later in life. Maybe you are one such person. If so, there are three Rs for you: Remember from where you have fallen, Repent of your sin and folly, and Return to the Father and do again the first works of love.

Be encouraged, saints, by the confession of the Apostle Paul in Philippians 3:12–14. He says:

'NOT that I have already obtained all of this, or have already been made perfect, but I press on to take hold of that for which Christ Jesus took hold of me. Brothers, I do not consider myself yet to have taken hold of it. But one thing that I do, forgetting what is behind and straining towards what is ahead, I press on toward the goal (gold) to win the prize for which God has called me heavenward in Christ Jesus.'

Finish strong, my brothers and sisters, so that we can also triumphantly declare like Paul in 2 Timothy 4:7, "I have fought the good fight, I have finished the race, I have kept the faith" (NIV). The crown of righteousness awaits. Finish strong and claim the prize.
PENNY DIS

Takeaway(s) / New Idea(s)

_____

_____

_____

_____

_____

Commitment(s)

_____

_____

_____

_____

_____

Prayer / Thanksgiving / Resolution(s)

_____

_____

_____

_____

_____

PENNY DIS

4

APATHY, SYMPATHY, AND EMPATHY

I have read of the great missionary Charles Greenaway, who once preached at a small Assemblies of God church some time ago. He shared passionately of the great need to share the gospel to the unreached people of Asia and of his own efforts doing so. Many were moved by the Holy Spirit. As was customary, after the message, a special offering was collected for the cause. As the offering plate was being passed around, there was a twelve-year-old boy named David Grant who was in tears as the plate approached him. He had no money to give, but he desperately wanted to do something. He made a strange request, asking the usher to place the offering plate on the floor. The bewildered usher reluctantly complied, and little David stood in it. "Jesus," he said. "I don't have any money, but you can have me." David Grant subsequently served as a missionary to India for decades.

This true story had me thinking of my responses (and that of people in general) to instances of need, which I encounter daily, namely responses of apathy, sympathy, and empathy. In response to the question, "Who is my neighbour?" Jesus told the well-known parable of The Good Samaritan in The Gospel of Saint Luke. A man was going down from Jerusalem to Jericho when he fell among thieves. They stopped him of his clothing, robbed him of his money, and beat him severely, almost to the point of death. A priest happened to be going down the same road, and when he saw the man, he passed by on the other side of the road. So too, a Levite when he came to the place, looked at him, and passed by on the other side. But a Samaritan, as he travelled, came where the man was, and he saw him in his need and had compassion on him. He went to him and bandaged his wounds, pouring on them oil and wine. He then put the man on his own donkey, took him to and inn and paid for his lodging and care, promising the innkeeper to pay for any additional costs incurred (Saint Luke10:30–36). It is a truly remarkable story.

If you and I will simply open our eyes, we will see myriads of needy people around us daily.

While I may not espouse the philosophy of the thieves: what is yours is mine; I cannot help but see myself in the priest and the Levite, whose philosophy was "what is mine is mine." The priest showed apathy or indifference. The Levite, at best, showed sympathy, but did nothing of significance to assist. The bowels of compassion of the Samaritan (hated and despised by Jews, and a wonderful type of Christ Himself) was moved to action, by empathy.

PENNY DIS

If you and I will simply open our eyes, we will see myriads of needy people around us daily. Let our vision not be impaired by apathy. Let us not soothe our conscience with sympathy but let us open our hearts and pocketbooks in empathy.
PENNY DIS

Takeaway(s) / New Idea(s)

_____

_____

_____

_____

_____

Commitment(s)

_____

_____

_____

_____

_____

Prayer / Thanksgiving / Resolution(s)

_____

_____

_____

_____

_____

PENNY DIS

5

WHO SINNED?

There has prevailed (even prior to Jesus' day) an erroneous view of God as it relates to sickness and human suffering. This is particularly so in cases of congenital illnesses. It must be God's punishment for human sin, some persist in believing.

After Job had suffered tremendous personal loss, even that of his beloved children and his health, his three friends, Eliphaz, Bildad, and Zophar skirted their baseless philosophy, until they finally came straight to the point, "Job, what sin have you committed?" Their understanding was simple and clearcut: the righteous are blessed by

God, and the unrighteous are punished by God.

Other parts of the Bible reflect the same view. In Psalm 73, one gets the impression that its author Asaph had nearly backslidden because of this same, erroneous way of thinking.

> "But as for me, my feet had almost slipped; I had nearly lost my foothold. For I envied the arrogant when I saw the prosperity of the wicked. They have no struggles; their bodies are healthy and strong. They are free from common human burdens; they are not plagued by human ills. Therefore pride is their necklace; they clothe themselves with violence... Surely in vain I have kept my heart pure and have washed my hands in innocence. All day long I have been afflicted, and every morning brings new punishments..." (NIV)

When I considered this view, it was oppressive to me until I entered the sanctuary of God. This was the AHA moment. It took getting into the presence of God and sensing the heart of God. Now, I am not so naive to deny that personal sin has severe consequences and God does step in to judge the sin of individuals and nations. Remember Sodom and Gomorrah and God's divine intervention when David sinned with Bathsheba? But far too often, we make the fatal error of assuming that all sickness and suffering constitute punishment from God.

Jesus' disciples did just that in Saint John 9. At the sight of the man who was born blind, they asked Jesus,

"Rabbi, who sinned, this man or his parents, that he was born blind?" Jesus corrected their erroneous thinking.

"Neither this man nor his parents sinned," said Jesus, "but this happened so that the works of God might be displayed in him.

Far too often, we make the fatal error of assuming that all sickness and suffering constitute punishment from God.

I am writing this meditation for two primary reasons:

#1 To correct this unbiblical philosophy that exists without and within the household of faith.

#2 Moreso, to encourage those who God has granted the gift of sickness or suffering who, like Job, have been enduring the brunt of misguided thinking.

I reinforce the words of Jesus: 'Neither this man nor his parents sinned but this happened that the works of God might be displayed in him.'

Dear child of God, keep on displaying God's glory and grace.

PENNY DIS

Takeaway(s) / New Idea(s)

___

___

___

___

___

Commitment(s)

___

___

___

___

___

Prayer / Thanksgiving / Resolution(s)

___

___

___

___

___

PENNY DIS

6

THE BLESSEDNESS OF BROKENNESS

We are broken people, every last one of us. We are sinful to the core and unable to save ourselves. But the benefit of being broken is that through the cracks, the light of the gospel of Jesus Christ can shine in. If a dwelling is shut tight with all windows and doors sealed (and without manmade light), it is a very dark place, devoid of the glory of God's wonderful sunlight. But what a magnificent difference when we deliberately open the windows and doors to let the sun (Son of God) shine in!

I remember once hearing about a man who was drowning at a beach one day. When his girlfriend on the shore realized that his frantic waves to her were not an indication of the wonderful time he was enjoying, but that he was instead in mortal danger. She ran in desperation to the lifeguard to put him on notice.

"My friend is drowning," she screamed at him. The lifeguard casually and calmly replied,

"I know," but seemed to do nothing but look intently at the futile efforts of her boyfriend's floundering. Perplexed by the lifeguard's noncommittal response, she raised her decibel level.

"You don't seem to understand. My friend is drowning," to which he again very calmly responded,

"I know." Just when the woman thought the lifeguard didn't care about her boyfriend losing his life, the lifeguard suddenly sprang into action, as the drowning man had stopped his floundering and submitted to fate. Utilizing all his skill and strength, the lifeguard brought the victim safely to the shore and resuscitated him. The girlfriend was thankful but bewildered at the lifeguard's delay.

"Why did you not respond when I first brought it to your attention?" He responded, "Your friend, though in a predicament, was still, by his own futile efforts, trying to save himself. If I went to his rescue then, we might both have perished as he grasped me in his desperation. When he had given up trying, it facilitated my saving him."

Jesus will not save us unless and until we recognize that we cannot save ourselves, no matter how we try. He saves us when we, in desperation, cry out to Him and trust Him completely to do what only He can do.

I was greatly encouraged by the testimony behind the writing of the great hymn "Just As I Am (Without One Plea)." Charlotte Elliott grew up in a Christian home, surrounded by family and deeply committed to their faith. As a young woman, she gained fame as a poet, showcasing her literary skills and wit. Despite her upbringing and success, she struggled with feelings of uselessness and depression, particularly after a serious illness left her disabled. "If God is good, able and loving (as I was brought up to believe), why is He allowing this to happen to me?" she thought.

Jesus will not save us unless and until we recognize that we cannot save ourselves, no matter how we try.

Charlotte Elliott grew angry at God and doubted the validity of her faith. In her time of turmoil, she encountered Swiss minister and hymnologist César Malan. She ranted on about her feelings of disbelief in the faith, to which he said nothing at first. When her rage had dissipated, he said, "Aren't you tired of your bondage to your anger? Do you not long to be set free?"

"How can I know the peace that you possess?" she asked. He told her it could only be found in the same God who she was vehemently resisting.

"How can I receive this peace?" she asked.

"Admit to Him your anger and frustration and come to Him just as you are. Humbly ask Him to forgive you?" She did just that and found that the Bread of Life satisfied the deep longings of her soul.

She later penned the words of the well-loved hymn.

Just As I Am, Without One Plea
"Just as I am, without one plea,
But that Thy blood was shed for me.
And that Thou bidst me come to Thee,
O Lamb of God, I come, I come."
~Charlotte Elliott

If (or since) you are broken and need mending, stop by the Great Potter's house. Give Him the fragments of your broken life, my friend. The Potter wants to put you back together again. Will you let Him?
PENNY DIS

Takeaway(s) / New Idea(s)

_____

_____

_____

_____

_____

Commitment(s)

_____

_____

_____

_____

Prayer / Thanksgiving / Resolution(s)

_____

_____

_____

_____

_____

7

EVEN IF YOU DON'T

Anyone can sing when the sun is shining bright, but you also need a song in your heart at night. I had heard of the term "sacrifice of praise" many times and often wondered what it truly referred to. Then, the Holy Spirit reminded me of Paul and Silas, who were severely beaten and were placed, hand and feet, in stocks in a dark, deep, damp, dusty, and disgusting dungeon in the city of Philippi. What was their crime? It was preaching Christ and delivering a slave girl who was demon possessed.

Instead of having a pity party, Paul and Silas lifted up their voices in prayer and praise to the Almighty. Acts 16:25

tells us, "Around midnight, Paul and Silas were praying and singing hymns to God" (ISV). "Suddenly, there was an earthquake so violent that the foundations of the prison were shaken. All the doors immediately flew open, and everyone's chains were unfastened" (Acts 16:26, ISV). When believers give praise to God at times that all hell is breaking loose, this is when praise is a sacrifice and a sweet aroma to God. When we do such, God is bound (I say this reverently) to respond on our behalf.

> Anyone can sing
> when the sun
> is shining bright,
> but you also
> need a song
> in your heart at night.

I remember fondly an embellishment that we made to the chorus "Hallelujah Anyhow" as young people at church. This was a Shelly Clark favourite.

Hallelujah Anyhow
"Hallelujah, anyhow, anyhow.
Never, never let your problems get you down.
When tribulations come your way,
Just lift your head up high and say,
'Pshaw!!!' Hallelujah, anyhow."

Job, in his darkest hour of trial, had lost his sheep, his camels, his donkeys, his livestock, his servants, and, as mentioned, his children, seven of them, all in the space of a few hours. The Lord even allowed Satan to take his health. From head to toe, he was covered with itchy, putrefying sores. Job's resolve: 'Though HE slay me, yet will I hope in [praise] Him.' Unbelievable!

In Daniel 3, Daniel's three Hebrew companions defied the decree of king Nebuchadnezzar, refusing to worship his golden image. The king was enraged by their defiance and gave them an ultimatum to obey or die in a fiery furnace made seven times hotter. With calm confidence, the tree responded, 'We are not afraid, O king, to answer you concerning this matter. We serve a God who is able to deliver us out of your hand. And even if *He* doesn't, be it known, O king, we will still not bow to your idol.' As a result, they were cast into the furnace, but they were protected by the fourth Man in the fire. They wouldn't bend, they wouldn't bow, and they wouldn't burn.

These youths had no doubt regarding God's ability to deliver, but they were also humbly submitted to God's sovereignty. 'We know YOU can, but even if YOU don't, we will still praise YOU.' This was very noteworthy. Job similarly intimated, "the Lord gave, and the Lord hath taken away; blessed be the name of the Lord" (Job 1:21, KJV).

My friend, is it possible that something unpleasant God has allowed in your life or something God has not granted you has left you upset and bitter toward God? Do you not realize that God is more concerned with your holiness than He is with your happiness? Are you making the nonsensical mistake that Peter made when he rebuked God about going to the cross? "Not so, Lord?" If Jesus is Lord (and He is), he is worthy of trust and praise, *always*, even when, in your eyes, He doesn't come through.

    Let us learn from the Hebrew young men and Job; let us allow God to be Lord of our lives. With natural eyes we may not see, but all is well that's done by Thee.

PENNY DIS

PENNY DIS

Takeaway(s) / New Idea(s)

_____

_____

_____

_____

_____

Commitment(s)

_____

_____

_____

_____

_____

Prayer / Thanksgiving / Resolution(s)

_____

_____

_____

_____

_____

8

SCARS IN HEAVEN?

The young Westpoint graduate had just passed training with flying colours. He finished top of his class. He wore the military uniform, shoes and buttons glistening, as he visited his hometown, a celebrity of sorts. Everybody wanted "a piece of him," to shake his hand, to embrace him.

Among the crowd that day was a decorated veteran in a wheelchair, amputated from his mid-thigh and with surgical pins holding every major bone left in place, a truly embattled soldier. He did not want to be a "wet blanket" or to rain on the newbie's parade. However, with tears in his eyes, he whispered in the young soldier's ears when he finally got the chance, "Soldier, where are your scars?"

He (forever) wears those scars for me!

From childhood, I (and maybe you too) have heard of the splendour of heaven: streets of pure gold; the New Jerusalem, 1000 cubits, cubed, hovering over the newly reassigned earth with no sea (I wonder why not); the Lamb-lighted eternal day; the river of life; the tree of life with perennial fruit; the golden thrones with Father and Son regally seated with the bride of Christ at His side; the floors of the throne room, of purest crystal... Eye has not seen, nor ear heard of its fullest magnificence. Oh, to see The Lord Jesus and the Father, the angelic hosts, the faithful of all ages, loved ones who have gone on before. What a reunion!

Only one thing that is manmade will be in that place: the scars of Calvary—The Lord's bruised brow, His nail-piercings (hands and feet), the spear wound at His side. This embattled loyal Soldier and Servant of Jehovah will gladly bear His battle scars, eternal reminders of the cost of our salvation. Isn't it ironic that we wretched and sinful recipients of God's amazing grace will be perfectly whole, while God's sinless, perfect Son will be forever scarred in heaven?

For me, for me, He (forever) wears those scars for me!

Praise the Saviour, Ye Who Know Him

"Praise the Saviour ye who know Him.
Who can say how much we owe Him?
Gladly let us render to Him
All we have and are!"
~Thomas Kelly

PENNY DIS

PENNY DIS

Takeaway(s) / New Idea(s)

_____

_____

_____

_____

_____

Commitment(s)

_____

_____

_____

_____

_____

Prayer / Thanksgiving / Resolution(s)

_____

_____

_____

_____

_____

9

LIFT YOUR HEAD UP HIGH, YOUR REDEMPTION DRAWS NIGH

Along a certain orbital path today, April 8, 2024, close to 300 million people from Mexico, USA, and Canada will be looking heavenward to behold a first-in-a-lifetime, or a once-in-a-lifetime, event, a total solar eclipse. For about three minutes, the shadow of the moon will perfectly cover the sun, turning day to night and back to day again. I just bought two pairs of eclipse shades so Sandra and I can look directly at the phenomenon (hope the clouds cooperate). Anticipation builds with each passing minute.

Niagara, Ontario seems to be one of the favoured viewing sites in Canada. This city is bracing for an unprecedented influx of over one million visitors from all over the world, who desire to experience this event adjacent to our world-renowned Niagara Falls (two juxtaposed natural wonders). I wish Niagara all the best, as their city is inundated and comes to a standstill.

A total solar eclipse is not a new phenomenon, but it is better understood and better predicted today. On Good Friday (or better still, on Passover), nearly 2000 years ago, as the Son of Man—Son of God was lifted on a Roman cross in humility and shame, one such solar event took place. A coincidence? I think not. Saint Luke 23:44–46 tells us that it was about the sixth hour (noon), and there was total darkness over all the earth until the ninth hour (3:00 p.m.). And the sun was darkened, and the veil of the temple "was rent in the midst." And when Jesus had cried with a loud voice "Tetelestai" (it is finished!!!), He said, "'Father, into thy hands I commend my spirit': and having said thus, he gave up the ghost" (Saint Luke 23:46, KJV).

Hatred was eclipsed by divine love.

The *Son* was rejected and murdered, and the *sun* refused to give its light. This was man at his worst and the Triune God at His best. Hatred was eclipsed by divine love.
PENNY DIS

PENNY DIS

Takeaway(s) / New Idea(s)

___

Commitment(s)

___

Prayer / Thanksgiving / Resolution(s)

___

10

LOOK UP!

Believers in Jesus Christ are encouraged to consider that the growing intensity of end-time signs should cause us to look up, for, redemption is coming. Look up for what? Rather, for whom?—For the triumphant return of the King of Kings Jesus Christ Himself (Saint Luke 21:28).

The day of Jesus's ascension was a sad day for Christ's followers. He had foretold them repeatedly that He had to return to The Father in heaven and he had promised to send the Holy Spirit. Reality left them heavyhearted and inconsolable. They could not imagine life without the tangible presence of The

Master. First, He was dead, then, gloriously alive, and now, He was leaving. Relive the scene with me, in Acts 1:9–11 (KJV):

> "And when he had spoken these things, while they beheld, he was taken up; and a cloud received him out of their sight. And while they looked steadfastly toward heaven as he went up, behold, two men stood by them in white apparel; Which also said, Ye men of Galilee, why stand ye gazing up into heaven? This same Jesus, which is taken up from you into heaven, shall so come in like manner as ye have seen him go into heaven."

Look up for what? Rather, for whom?

For those who do not know, The Lord's return will occur in two phases: the "secret coming" (the rapture) to take believers to heaven mentioned in 1 Thessalonians 4:13–17 and reiterated in 1 Corinthians 15:50–55, and His global, visible coming to earth to destroy and judge His enemies and establish His kingdom. (Also read Jude 14–15 and Revelation 19:11–21.) So, both secretly and publicly, Jesus Christ is coming again, and soon. And they (particularly unbelieving Jews) shall look upon Him whom they have pierced and shall weep and mourn (Zechariah 12:10).

You can say all you want to say now, but on that day, Christ will have the final and irrefutable word. Read about the final human judgment in Revelation 20:11–15. Verse 15 says, "And whosoever was not found written in the book of life was cast into the lake of fire" (KJV). Yes, my friend, hell is real, and I pray it won't be your final dwelling.

Believers in Christ, this is not a time for slumber nor idleness, for now is our salvation closer than when we first believed (Romans 13:11). "Blessed *are* those servants, whom the lord when he cometh shall find watching" (Saint Luke 12:37, KJV). Lift your head up! Redemption draws nigh.
PENNY DIS

PENNY DIS

Takeaway(s) / New Idea(s)

_____

_____

_____

_____

_____

Commitment(s)

_____

_____

_____

_____

_____

Prayer / Thanksgiving / Resolution(s)

_____

_____

_____

_____

_____

11

CHILDISH OR CHILDLIKE?

Child*ish* or child*like*? I once thought these adjectives were synonymous, but I have come to learn that they are worlds apart. Do you remember when you were a child? Some of us will need to rewind several decades down memory lane, for sure. Do you recall how exasperated you were when you did not get something that you really, really wanted, when you wanted it? The tears, the tantrums, the vexation and malice, the anger... That's childish, and those were not your shining hours.

I remember getting two good slaps on my seat of correction (buttocks) and was instantly cured of my malady. They call this child abuse these days. (Much learning has made us mad.)

I have heard that many psychologists who seek to understand human nature study the behaviour of children. As we grow older, we learn to control our natural tendencies of youth to some measure, but a child follows instinct.

In 1 Corinthians 13 (the love chapter), Paul says, in verse 11, "When I was a child, I spoke as a child, I understood as a child, I thought as a child; but when I became a man, I put away childish things" (NKJV). Paul learned to move on from childishness. Unfortunately, some of us never do. As we can see from the Bible's instruction, it is expected that we will outgrow childishness. What God (and others) hope we will not outgrow is child*like*ness.

I remember hearing about the young children of a friend. They were experiencing a power outage one dark night after he tucked them into bed. The house got very dark and eerily quiet in an instant.

"Daddy!!!", the three girls screamed, almost in unison.

"Don't be afraid girls! Daddy is here! Go back to sleep!" the father replied. That's exactly what these reassured girls did. They were childlike, trusting Daddy completely.

"When I was a child, I spoke as a child, I understood as a child, I thought as a child; but when I became a man, I put away childish things"
(1 Corinthians 13:11, NKJV).

I also heard of a little girl who was trapped on the third floor of her home, which was on fire on a dark night. The firefighters were on scene below the child's bedroom window. The little girl's only chance for survival was to jump out of the window into the safety net set below. She heard their voices but saw nothing but darkness. Her father also encouraged her to jump, but the child was afraid.

"I can't see you, Daddy."

"Honey, you know how much Daddy loves you, don't you?"

"Yes Daddy", she replied, fighting back the tears.

"Then please jump, I will catch you," the faither said. Fully persuaded, the little girl closed her eyes and jumped. Her life was saved that night: childlikeness.

One day, the arrogant disciples were arguing which of them was the greatest. (They had never heard of Muhammad Ali!). These followers of Jesus should have known better, after walking with Greatness for nearly three years. I just love what Jesus did. In Saint Matthew 18:2–4 we read, 'Then Jesus called a child to Him, and set him in the midst of them, and said, Assuredly I say to you, unless you are converted and become as little children, you will by no means enter the kingdom of heaven. Therefore, whoever humbles himself as this little child is the greatest.' What an object lesson! That surely ended the debate, even if they had not completely learned the lesson. How do I know they might not have completely learned the lesson? Well, just look at what transpired a few weeks later at The Last Supper. It was the responsibility of the first disciple to arrive to wash his feet and to wash the feet of the others who arrived later also. Nobody did it. Can you imagine the baker's dozen (thirteen) of them reclining around a low table with dirty, smelly feet almost in each other's faces.? Once again, Jesus had to give them another lesson in humility and the spirit of childlikeness by washing their feet Himself.

If you are still exhibiting childishness, grow up in God, and leave this behind. If the cares of this life have evaporated the pure joy of childlike fervour, I pray you will rediscover it. Some have unfortunately been robbed of their childhood. Run like a child to the arms of your heavenly Father and let Him assure you how much your Daddy loves you.
PENNY DIS

PENNY DIS

Takeaway(s) / New Idea(s)

_____

_____

_____

_____

_____

Commitment(s)

_____

_____

_____

_____

_____

Prayer / Thanksgiving / Resolution(s)

_____

_____

_____

_____

_____

12

THE GIFT OF THE PRESENT

The good old days—many idolize them. As good as they might have been, they were fraught with flaws. Life expectancy was low. Infant mortality and mothers dying in childbirth were high. Education and job opportunities were limited. Moral indiscretions were still in existence, but skeletons were hidden deep in closets, and mum was the word. Many a child grew up never knowing who their father was; speaking about their conception was anathema. If we are honest, the good old days were not as good as some would have us believe.

Yesterday is gone. Learn the lessons taught, but don't dwell there.

Move on. Don't perennially relive past failures, and certainly don't let them define you. You are not trapped in your past like "untouchables" of the Indian caste system, without any possibility of escape. If you have sinned, repent, confess your sins to Jesus, and forsake them. Forgiveness is available; this is what Good Friday and Resurrection Sunday are about. If you have been hurt or abused in the past, forgive and let Jesus show you how much you are loved and valued by Him. For heaven's sake (and yours), don't live in yesterday.

> Yesterday is gone. Learn the lessons taught, but don't dwell there.

Then, there is the other end of the spectrum. Your yesterdays may have resulted in great personal success and achievement. You might be able to look back with great pride, but you too cannot afford to dwell there. There are other mountains to conquer and castles to build. It has been rightly said that the enemy of the best is the good. We, at times, fail to achieve the best because we are too easily satisfied with the good. It's time to press on.

The Apostle Paul puts it this way in Philippians 3:13–14:

> 'Brethren, I do not count myself to have apprehended: but this one thing I do, forgetting those things which are behind, and reaching forward to those things which are ahead, I press toward [forward]...'

Periodically reflect on yesterday, then press on.

It has been said by some that some Christians are so heavenly minded that they are of no earthly good. The opposite might be the more often the reality—some Christians are so earthly minded that they are of no heavenly good. But let us not too quickly dismiss the kernel of truth in the former statement. This is not new. I understand that early Christians, in ignorance, anticipating the imminent return of Christ, sold their possessions and lived in enclaves in the hills, simply waiting for The Lord to come and take them to heaven. They lived only for the future, ignoring the wondrous gift of the present. If a pregnant woman only lived for the delivery of her unborn, she would have missed out on the wonder of the process and the beauty of bonding with this miraculous life in her womb. Nine months would have been wasted. If you are presently between jobs, and you live only for the next period of employment, you may end up wasting days, weeks, months, and even years of your life. What about the now?

God gave Joseph promises in dreams of his future elevation and deliverance of his family, but these took nearly twenty years to be fulfilled. He would have wasted two decades of his life if he was only living for the future. Abraham was promised that he would be the father of many nations, but this was twenty-five years in the making—a quarter century could have been wasted.

Nothing is written in scripture about Jesus between the ages of twelve and (approximately) thirty. What was He doing all this time, only killing eighteen years in anticipation of His ministry? I am sure there were day-to-day opportunities to build relationships with

His Father, His family, and His community. Saint Luke 2:52 states, "Jesus grew in wisdom and in stature and in favor with God and all the people (NLT)." Yes, while Jesus anticipated His future ministry, He never overlooked present opportunities.

The past is gone, the future is not yet, so we come to the gift of the present. What is God doing in you and for you now? What are you doing daily to make His glory known? You won't want to miss what God has for you in the now. If you can, listen to Jeremy Camp's song "Keep Me In The Moment" and be inspired and blessed. I don't want you to miss what God has for you.

Yesterday is gone. Forget it. Tomorrow is not promised. Plan tentatively for it. Today is here, maximize it.

PENNY DIS

PENNY DIS

Takeaway(s) / New Idea(s)

_____

_____

_____

_____

_____

Commitment(s)

_____

_____

_____

_____

_____

Prayer / Thanksgiving / Resolution(s)

_____

_____

_____

_____

_____

13

MAN ON THE MIDDLE CROSS

Saint Matthew 27:26,38 describes how Pontius Pilate released Barabbas and delivered Jesus, when he had scourged Him, to be crucified. Then two thieves (possibly murderers) were crucified with Him, one on the right and the other on the left. Listen, if you can, to the song "Man On The Middle Cross" by Rhett Walker. Crucifixion was the Roman's way of dealing with enemies of the state, setting examples as a deterrent to all and sundry who would dare to oppose them. Fall in line or else... Imagine being whipped almost to the point of death and then being suspended on a cross, with your entire body weight borne by spikes in your wrists and through your ankles. This was cruelty at its worst, and Roman soldiers perfected this to an art. Sometimes death would take days.

Three men were crucified on that fateful day nearly 2000 years ago on a hill outside of Jerusalem at a place called "The Place of the skull." Two were dangerous criminals who were possibly cohorts of Barabbas (a notorious insurrectionist), men deserving of death. But what of the Man on the middle cross? Who is He, and what has He done? Why was such hostility and human venom meted out to Him?

Just over three decades prior, the angel Gabriel visited a young maiden called Mary (possibly in her mid-teens) foretelling her virgin birthing of the Messiah (Saint Luke 1:26–38). Several months later, angels proclaimed the birth of Emmanuel (God with us) to shepherds in the fields of Bethlehem at night. (Saint Luke 2:1–14). Several decades later, John the Baptist identified Him (Emmanuel—Jesus) by the Jordan River as "the Lamb of God" (Saint John 1:29). God Himself spoke from heaven at His baptism "You are My beloved Son; in You I am well pleased" (Saint Luke 3:22, NKJV).

"Truly this was the Son of God!" (Saint Mattew 27:54, KJV).

Simon Peter acknowledged Him to be the Christ, the son of the living God (Saint John 6:69). Thomas, when Jesus appeared to the twelve, days after His resurrection, avowed Him to be Lord and God (and he was not swearing as some would have us believe) (Saint John 20:27–28). Judas, after betraying Him, had a change of heart, declaring Him to be innocent (Saint Matthew 27:4). Pilate prosecuted Him and found Him to be without fault. Pilate's wife warned Pilate not to have anything to do with the harm of this just Man (Saint Matthew 27:19). One thief on the cross (as to whether he was on the left or right, only heaven will tell) said of Jesus, 'He has done nothing amiss' (Saint Luke 23:40). The Roman centurion who oversaw His crucifixion, when he saw the hours of darkness and the subsequent earthquake, he feared greatly saying "Truly this was the Son of God!" (Saint Mattew 27:54, KJV).

Jesus, during His ministry, did nothing but good. He healed the sick, exorcised away demons, gave sight to the blind, raised up the lame, fed the hungry, even raised the dead. Why then was the common criminal Barabbas released and He crucified? Was this a haphazard event? Was it simply a travesty of justice? A thousand times NO!!!! It was the pre-determined plan of God for the redemption of all who would believe. Isaiah's prophesy was 700 years before the event. Read with me, Isaiah 53:5–6 (KJV) says, "But he was wounded for our transgressions, he was bruised for our iniquities: the chastisement of our peace was upon him; and with his stripes we are healed. All we like sheep have gone astray; we have turned every one to his own way; and the Lord hath laid on him the iniquity of us all." Isaiah 53:10 says, "Yet it pleased the Lord to bruise Him..." WHAT!!!? The Father put His beloved Son to death? How can this be?—It was for you and me.

The words of some hymns come to mind.

O Blessed Lord, What Hast Thou Done?

"O blessed Lord, what hast Thou done!
How vast a ransom paid!
Who could conceive God's only Son
Upon the altar laid!"

~ Mary Peters

It Is Well with My Soul

"My sin, oh, the bliss of this glorious thought!
My sin, not in part but the whole,
Is nailed to the cross, and I bear it no more,
Praise The Lord, praise The Lord, O my soul!"

~ Daniel Warner

My only response to all of this is to fall prostrate on my face, repenting, receiving and rejoicing. I truly thank God for the Man on the middle cross. Hallelujah. Praise The Lord.
PENNY DIS

PENNY DIS

Takeaway(s) / New Idea(s)

_____

_____

_____

_____

_____

Commitment(s)

_____

_____

_____

_____

_____

Prayer / Thanksgiving / Resolution(s)

_____

_____

_____

_____

_____

14

FULLY KNOWN, FULLY LOVED

Back in Shakespearean days, it was not uncommon for one person to play the part of more than one character on stage. To carry this out this feat, the actor would use distinctive masks for each character. It is from this phenomenon that we get the word "hypocrite" (or two-faced). Some of us have mastered the art of being two-faced. We can be one person, say at church, and be a completely different character at home. I am sure we all are familiar with at least one person who rendered us incredulous about some outrageous act of theirs, which was totally out of character. *"This is not the person that I know,"* you must have thought.

Some of us have mastered the art of being two-faced.

Maybe you have been desperately trying to be the person that loved ones want you to be, and you want to impress and not disappoint them, but their expectation is not who you are. You are tired of the pretence, but you fear if they knew you, they would not love you anymore. Can I tell you something? There is One who knows everything about you, even your deepest, darkest, most disgusting deeds and thoughts, yet loves you passionately. His name is Jesus Christ.

In Saint John chapter 4, we read of Jesus' encounter and discourse with a woman at Sychar's well who had a despicable past (and present) and was living a secret life. Her name is not revealed, but it was quite strange for her to be coming to the well in the midday heat. Most of the women (and it was women in that culture who fetched water for their households) came in the early morning or late afternoon to do so. Perhaps she came at the time she did to avoid the stares and sneers of others who knew her history and sins. She had been married five times and was currently living with another woman's husband. Many of the likes of Hollywood had nothing over this woman.

I wonder what she thought as she saw this strange man in the distance, sitting on the well? She was familiar with men. Would He be any different? Jesus started the conversation on the topic of water (a sensible way to begin engaging). Jesus said to her "Give Me a drink" (Saint John 4:7, ESV). She was startled by His request, and rightly so.

"'How is it that you, a Jew, ask for a drink from me, a woman of Samaria?" (For Jews have no dealings with Samaritans.)' (Saint John 4:9, ESV). You see, Jews saw Samaritans as "half-breeds" in the derogatory sense; they were Jews who intermarried with Gentiles. Jews detested them, seeing them just as they saw Gentiles, as dogs. Jews would rather walk twice the distance of their journey to avoid contact with Samaritans, yet Jesus told

His disciples that He must go through Samaria (for He had a divine appointment with this woman). Back to the conversation. Jesus offered the woman a divinely superior spiritual thirst quencher.

Jesus answered her, "If you knew the gift of God, and who it is that is saying to you, 'Give me a drink,' you would have asked him, and he would have given you living water" (Saint John 4:10, ESV).

She misunderstood. "Sir, you have nothing to draw water with, and the well is deep. Where do you get that living water?" (Saint John 4:11, ESV). She then engages in religious small talk. 'Are you greater than our father Jacob [who gave us this well]?' (Saint John 4:12, ESV).

Jesus rebutted, " Everyone who drinks of this water will be thirsty again, but whoever drinks of the water that I will give him will never be thirsty again" (Saint John 4:13–14, ESV). She is interested in His offer, though she obviously does not understand what He means.

"Sir, give me this water, so that I will not be thirsty or have to come here to draw water" (Saint John 4:15, ESV). Then Jesus cuts to the chase.

"Go, call your husband, and come here" (Saint John 4:16, ESV). I can just imagine her surprise, guilt, and shame.

"I have no husband," she said (Saint John 4:17, ESV). Jesus commends her honesty.

'You have rightly said that you have no husband. You have had five husbands and the man you are living with is not your husband but another woman's,' Jesus said (Saint John 4:17). She was shocked. *How could He possibly have known this about me?*" She tried to change the subject.

"Sir, I perceive that You are a prophet," she said. (Saint John 4:19, ESV). Then she went back to her religious chit chat. How we sinners love to hide behind our religiosity? "I know that Messiah is coming (he who is called Christ). When he comes, he will tell us all things" (Saint John 14:25, ESV). Then He drops the bomb.

"I who speak to you AM HE" (Saint John 14:26, ESV). What a revelation! Her spiritual eyes were instantly opened, and she perceived Messiah face to face. She dropped her water jug. She was no longer interested in water from a well; she had drunk of the Water of life.

The Samaritan woman at the well was totally consumed with the non-judgmental, all-loving Man from Galilee, who knew the worst about her and yet had received her. *He knows me, and He loves me*, she must have thought. Will you surrender to this unspeakable love, like this woman, unnamed and messed up in the eyes of many? Jesus will give you living water that was not in the well. Well, well, well.
PENNY DIS

Takeaway(s) / New Idea(s)

_____

_____

_____

_____

_____

Commitment(s)

_____

_____

_____

_____

_____

Prayer / Thanksgiving / Resolution(s)

_____

_____

_____

_____

_____

PENNY DIS

15

PAST YOUR PAST

Although I had a passion for mathematics, I was merely average in my physics performance. Mechanics was the only strand in physics in which I prospered, as it closely resembled math to me. I was intrigued by the vector quantities displacement, velocity, and acceleration. I found that a body may initially have a negative displacement, but by having a positive velocity and positive acceleration, it was only a matter of time before the displacement became positive. What was most influential was not the displacement (initial location) being negative, but the velocity and acceleration (direction and rate of motion) being positive.

Many of us came into the world with tons of baggage, including an ungodly and embarrassing heritage, which we did not want and could not change. I once heard of a man that shook his family tree and down fell some assorted nuts. Another man, I heard, traced his ancestry, promising his mother that he would truthfully write about each person he discovered. Then he found a great, great uncle who was a notorious serial killer who was executed by the electric chair by the state, and he was in a quandary. How was he to represent this embarrassing antecedent? He wrote, "MY great, great uncle Fred was a very popular man. He once held a government chair. His death came as a great shock."

We may sometimes come from humble beginnings or even from disgraceful ones. You wish you could forget the past. I am here to tell you, your ancestry or your start in life does not have to define you.

It is not where you have been, or even where you are that matters, it is where you are heading, particularly if the Good and Great Shepherd is leading you.

Your ancestry or your start in life does not have to define you.

Your past need not define you if you find your identity in your Creator and Lord.

Abraham was a pagan idolater when the Sovereign God called him from Ur of the Chaldeans. He believed and walked with God by faith (though not perfectly) and became the father of the faithful, and God's friend, even the progenitor of the Messiah Jesus the Christ. Jacob was a swindler of no mean order, the younger twin from a very dysfunctional family. He duped his elder twin out of a birthright and blessing, even lying and taking advantage of his father's blindness. Though his faults were many, God knew that deep down, he loved The Lord. Imagine, God even dared to refer Himself as the God of Jacob. Absolutely amazing! What grace!

Rahab made her living by selling her body to dirty-minded and lustful-hearted men on the walls of Jericho. She, however, hid the two Israeli spies and showed them kindness. She not only delivered her life, but those of her household as well, when in obedience she put that scarlet thread in her window when Israel later attacked and routed Jericho. (What a beautiful type of the redemption by blood through the Passover Lamb). Rahab, graciously, is in the genealogy of the Messiah (Read Saint Matthew 1:5), and she receives honorary mention for her faith in Hebrews 11: 31. I wondered for a long time why she was referred to as Rahab the harlot, even after her conversion. It was later revealed to me that it was not highlighting her despicable past but rather the abundance of God's grace to save.

Ruth was a Moabitess, descendant of the incestuous elder daughter of Lot (Genesis 19:30–37).
Imagine having this as your ancestry? What disgrace!
The nation of Moab was cursed by God (Numbers 21: 9), synonymous with spiritual whoredom (Numbers 25:1), referred to as God's "washpot" (Psalm 60:8, KJV). Yet despite all this, Ruth found

and clave to the God of Israel and obtained redemption. One cannot forget her famous words, "Entreat me not to leave you, Or to turn back from following after you; For wherever you go, I will go; And wherever you lodge, I will lodge; Your people shall be my people, And your God, my God" (Ruth 1:16, NKJV). WOW. Ruth is also in the genealogy of The Lord Jesus Christ (Saint Matthew 1:5).

    My brother, sister, or friend, I trust that this word from The Lord encourages you. Your past need not define you if you'll let Jesus take you past your past. PENNY DIS

PENNY DIS

Takeaway(s) / New Idea(s)

_____

_____

_____

_____

_____

Commitment(s)

_____

_____

_____

_____

_____

Prayer / Thanksgiving / Resolution(s)

_____

_____

_____

_____

_____

16

WOUNDED SOLDIER, BATTLE ON

Devoted followers of Christ will, from time to time, go through seasons when (according to Murphy's law) everything that can go wrong does just that: your marriage, your job, your health, your finances, your children, your ministry, your self-esteem—you name it. They all capitulate, and all that is left is ashes. You may wonder, *God, are You still there, and do you still love me?*" Guess what? He is, and He does!

The Chistian life does not insulate the believer from the troubles and trials of everyday life. In fact, there will be times that it invites such hardships. Jesus calls us to deny self, take up a cross (not a frisbee), and possibly die for the cause. We have been enlisted for spiritual war and not a Sunday School picnic.

2 Timothy 2:3 encourages us to endure hardness as good soldiers of Jesus Christ. When we go through the difficult times, we might be tempted to think that ours is the worst, or we are the only ones. Let us consider what a few have endured in the biblical past. There was Job. The Sabaeans attacked and captured his oxen and donkeys, killed the attending servants, and only one survived to tell the tale. While he was yet speaking, another servant came with another tale of woe. The fire of God (or so he thought) fell from the sky and burned up the sheep and the servants, and he alone escaped to tell the fate. While he was still speaking, another servant came relating that the Chaldeans swept down and raided his camels, killed the attending servants, and he alone survived to tell the tale. While he was still speaking, another messenger of woe came. Can you believe this? (Fact can, at times, be stranger than fiction.) His sons and daughters were eating and drinking in

the eldest brother's house, and suddenly, a mighty wind swept in from the desert and struck the four corners of the house. It collapsed on them, and they died. The messenger was the only one to survive to tell the tale. All this… in a matter of hours. And you and I think we are the only ones with hardships? Job's response is heartbreaking and yet inspiring. He tore his robe in grief, shaved his head, fell to his knees, and worshipped. He said, "The Lord gave, and the Lord hath taken away; blessed be the name of the Lord" (Job 1:21, KJV). WOW!

The Chistian life does not insulate the believer from the troubles and trials of everyday life.

There was David. There was a period in David's life when, in self-exile to escape the jealous and self-seeking King Saul, he lived among the Philistines, the lifelong enemies of Israel. He had to flee home, family and country. Though anointed by Samuel to be the next king of Israel, he was on the run and hunted like a dog. To show that he was not a threat to the Philistines, David sought to join the Philistine army in battle against Israel (I find this very strange), but was rejected by the commanding generals who did not fully trust him. On David's return with his men to their camp in Ziklag, tired and hungry after three days marching, they saw that the city was on fire. The Amalekites raided the defenceless city and burned it after taking captive all the women and children. David and his men were heartbroken and filled with grief. David's men sought to take out their anger on their revered leader David, as they could not come to grips with their loss of wives and children. In their grief and irrationality, they were going to stone David. David must have wondered to himself, *What next, Lord?* David and his men, we are told, wept until they had no more strength to weep. In the midst of the mutiny, we read that David encouraged himself in The Lord, his God. I believe he had a powerful time of devotion in The Lord's presence. Out of His troubles, David said this, "The Lord is my shepherd; I shall not want... Surely goodness and mercy shall follow me all the days of my life: and I will dwell in the house of the Lord for ever" (Psalm 23:1,6).

Before battling, David sought The Lord. 'Shall we pursue?'

God said 'pursue.'

David asked, 'Will we overtake?'

God answered, 'Yes, you will overtake.'

Finally, David asked, 'Will we recover?'

God was emphatic, 'You shall recover all.' So, David did, and God was true to His word; David recovered all.

Job and David knew that their God would not fail them despite their difficult times. So, are you going through one of those difficult seasons right now? God told me to tell you something. Things may look hopeless, but if you, like Job and David, though wounded, will battle on, even if you don't understand what God is doing, then, though the battle is hot, victory is sure.

Hallelujah.

PENNY DIS

PENNY DIS

Takeaway(s) / New Idea(s)

_____

_____

_____

_____

_____

Commitment(s)

_____

_____

_____

_____

_____

Prayer / Thanksgiving / Resolution(s)

_____

_____

_____

_____

_____

17

GOD'S NOT DONE WITH YOU

Simon Peter often failed to put his brain in gear before putting his tongue in motion. One moment, he declared a bedrock truth, "Thou art the Christ, The Son of The Living God," and the next, he was rebuking Jesus when He said He was to die on a Roman cross (Saint Matthew 16:16; 16:22–23, KJV). Jesus had to rebuke the devil who was using Peter as a detraction from His main purpose, "Get thee behind me, Satan: thou art an offence unto me: for thou savourest not the things that be of God, but those that be of men" (Saint Matthew 16:23, KJV). Talk about going "from hero to zero!" When Jesus prophesied to Peter of His oncoming denial of Christ, Peter was indignant. 'These others may deny You Lord, but I Peter bar Jonas will NEVER do such a thing." Jesus told him, "Peter, Satan has desired to have you, to sift you like wheat. But I have prayed for you. When you are converted (have repented), strengthen the brethren.' When Peter's test came, he failed miserably, as prophesied. When immediately afterward his and Jesus' eyes "made four", Peter remembered what Jesus had said and ran off into the night shadows and wept bitterly. Surely, it was over for him.

John Mark was a spiritually promising young man, growing leaps and bounds in the things of God. He was cousin to Barnabas, Paul's ministry partner at Antioch. When the Spirit, after many days of prayer and fasting, led the elders at the Antioch Assembly to commend Barnabas and Paul to missionary service, Barnabas suggested that they take John Mark with them. Paul agreed. When the going got tough on that first missionary journey, John Mark abandoned ship, returning to the comforts of life in Jerusalem. Barnabas was understanding (maybe because he was John Mark's relative). Paul was not amused.

Later, when Barnabas suggested that he and Paul should follow up with the believers they met on the first missions' trip, Paul agreed. When Barnabas suggested, however, that they give John Mark a second chance, Paul vehemently objected. I imagine the conversation went something like this:

'Not over my dead body! I will not have anything to do with that sellout.'

'Give the young man a break Paul.'

'No way, Barnabas! Never again!'

Barnabas said, 'But brother Paul, remember how I stuck up for you when you were first saved, and the apostles at Jerusalem thought you were not sincere.' The Bible said, when there was no small dissention between the two missionaries (in other words, when the two almost came to blows), they parted ways. Barnabas went one way with John Mark, and Paul chose another partner (Silas) and went another way. We are talking apostle and chief deacon here, you know. The Bible did not pretty this up, but rather told it like it was. John Mark must have been devastated.

PENNY DIS

I thank God that He gives second, third, fourth, and nth chances. Where would we be if it wasn't for grace? I have "blown it" so many times, but each time that I repent, He forgives me, welcomes me, and uses me again. Grace is greater than all my sin. Amazing!

Where would we be if it wasn't for grace?

Peter repented, and preached the first gospel message, resulting in the conversion of three thousand souls on the Day of Pentecost. John Mark was later sent for by Paul, of all people, who then found him to be profitable to serve with him in ministry. John Mark was moved by the Holy Spirit to pen the gospel of Saint Mark.

So, you have messed up AGAIN. Do you have mere remorse, or are you genuinely repentant? Are you merely embarrassed because your halo has fallen, or are you broken because of the manner in which your sin hurt God? If the answers to these are the latter—if you are teachable—God will instruct you,

and as long as you are malleable, God will continue to conform you to the image of His Son, Jesus. Don't hide. Don't run, for God's not done with you.
PRAISE THE LORD!
HALLELUJAH!
PENNY DIS

PENNY DIS

Takeaway(s) / New Idea(s)

_____

_____

_____

_____

_____

Commitment(s)

_____

_____

_____

_____

Prayer / Thanksgiving / Resolution(s)

_____

_____

_____

_____

_____

18

TRUTH BE TOLD

It has been said, "Speak the truth and speak it ever; cost it what it will. He (or she) who hides the wrong he does, does the wrong thing still." This is one of the gems that we had to commit to memory as a child in elementary school. Do they teach these moral values in schools to children these days? I just watched a BBC documentary on Rolex watch-grabbers in contemporary London. Young people would stalk and rob (sometimes at gunpoint) victims with pricy watches on their wrists, selling the loot online to the highest bidder. When asked by undercover journalists if they had any remorse for such heinous activity, many had none whatsoever. Some of them said, 'You gotta do what you gotta do.' It was all about doing what it takes to achieve the desired lifestyle.

Many of today's youth have no concept of right and wrong, but are they solely to be blamed? No. Their parents and the other adults in their lives may have never inculcated these values in them in their childhood or never consistently modelled them.

Speak the truth

and speak it ever;

cost it what it will.

He (or she) who hides the wrong he

does, does the wrong thing still."

The phone rings, and your child answers. It's for you, but it's that boorish woman who does not know when to stop chatting. You have no time for such, at least not now. "Tell her I'm not home," you say. What are you teaching this child? Did you hear about the silly child who (in a similar situation) told the person on the line, "Mommy said to tell you that she is not at home." Truth be told, far too often the truth is not being told, who really speaks the truth these days? Not politicians!

You know that many politicians are lying every time their lips move. They make promises they have no intentions of keeping, and the public is so gullible that they believe them. When some are elected, they change the laws, making it nigh impossible to remove them.

Not social media. Daily social media spews out a lot of lies and deceptions—fake news. Some of the pictures aren't real. The perfect body parts aren't real. The faultless relationships aren't real. All this fabrication is intended to make your reasonable life appear so abhorrent that the influencers' lives of misery have company. Smiling faces (many times) tell lies.

Not the advertisers putting out inflated percentages of success, inflating prices, making super profits. Commodities are not being sold for what they are worth, but rather for what they can bamboozle consumers into paying for them.

Not the evolutionary scientists. These insist on making monkeys of themselves and simpletons that they can fool. This is devolution. The Bible says mankind is created in the image of God. Evolutionists try to "educate" us by telling us that we are descendants of apes. Whose report will you believe? And how do they verify millions and trillions of years? Carbon 14 dating systems assume that everything that is happening today has always happened at the same rate. What about the worldwide flood, which is mentioned in almost every culture, no matter how unsophisticated? Would that not affect the scheme and order of things?

Now, the intellectual powers that be are wanting to convince us that there is no absolute or objective truth. Truth, they say, is relative and subjective. You hear today of people espousing their truth, and you are encouraged to speak yours. No wonder the world is in the mess and chaos it is.

This is not new, however. There was a time in biblical Israel when they had no king, and every man did what was right in his own eyes (Judges 21:25). Israel was at an all-time low.

Sadly, we can't rely on pastors and teachers of God's Word to consistently espouse the truth. Some are men-pleasers, condoning actions that God has clearly condemned. Are they ignorant (for example) of God's judgment on the evil twin cities of Sodom and Gomorrah? But then, scripture warned that these perilous last day events would come. 'For men will not always endure (accept) the truth, but will surround themselves with teachers, having itching ears, who will tell them what their sinful fleshly appetites want to hear' (2 Timothy 4:3).

What is truth? Pilate asked Jesus this question as Christ stood before him in judgment. Truth stood before Pontius Pilate, and he didn't recognize it. How sad! Jesus Christ unapologetically stated about Himself in Saint John 14:6 "I am the way, the truth, and the life. No one comes to the Father except through Me" (NKJV). Notice that He did not say a way, a truth or a life. He is the only way, the only truth and the only source of eternal life. "For there is one God, and one mediator between God and men, the man Christ Jesus" (1 Timothy 2:5, KJV). I dare say that Jesus does not approve of contemporary political correctness as it pertains to religious tolerance and inclusiveness. All other self-proclaimed "messiahs" that came before (or after), He called "thieves" and "robbers" (Saint John 10:8).

The Word of God (the Bible) is also truth. Psalm 19:9 says, 'The judgments (words of God) are true and righteous altogether.' Psalm 119:160 reiterates, "Thy word *is* true *from* the beginning: and every one of thy righteous judgments *endureth* for ever" (KJV). In Jesus' High-Priestly prayer (Saint John 17:17), Jesus besought the Father, "Sanctify them by Your truth. Your word is truth." Romans 3:4 encourages us, "Even if everyone else is a liar, God is true" (NLT). MY friend, if God says X and man says Y, believe X, for God is not a man that He should lie (Numbers 23:19). Hebrews 6:18 reminds us that not only does God not lie, but He cannot lie; it is outside the realm of possibility for Him to do so. Furthermore, since our Father is the God of truth, it is incumbent on us as His children to speak truthfully. Ephesians 4:25 says, "Therefore, putting away lying, 'Let each one of you speak truth with his neighbor,'" (NKJV). Colossians 3:9 endorses, "Do not lie to one another, since you have put off the old man with his deeds" (NKJV).

Satan is referred to as "the father of lies" (Saint John 8:44). If lying is your habit, then you make it abundantly clear who your father is. Like father, like son (or daughter). Since you and I (or at least I hope *you* and I) believe in the name the name of Christ, then let us manifest the nature of Christ in truth-telling. Truth be told, let the truth be told.
PENNY DIS

Takeaway(s) / New Idea(s)

_____

_____

_____

_____

_____

Commitment(s)

_____

_____

_____

_____

_____

Prayer / Thanksgiving / Resolution(s)

_____

_____

_____

_____

_____

19

OUT OF MY HANDS, INTO YOURS

Like the control freak Jacob in the Bible, some of us, though believers in Jesus, can be so self-willed; demanding to have our way instead of submitting to His. Jacob had godly desires but sought to fulfil them by fleshly means. He esteemed the birthright (which God had promised would be his) and the attendant blessing but achieved it by bribing his vulnerable twin brother and by deceiving his blind father.

As a result of his devious actions, he had to run away from his angry twin who sought to murder him. On route to his mother's homeland, he had his first encounter with God at Bethel. In a dream, he saw a ladder that went from heaven to earth and saw angels both ascending and descending upon the ladder. He recognized he had a divine visitation from God. He made a vow to God, saying, "If God will be with me, and will keep me in this way that I go, and will give me bread to eat, and raiment to put on, so that I come again to my father's house in peace; then shall the LORD be my God" (Genesis 28:20–21, KJV).

In the person of his uncle Laban (his mother's brother), Jacob found a greater deceiver than himself. (God *does* have a sense of humour.) Deception appeared to be in the genes of his mother's family line, not skipping a generation. Laban tricked Jacob into marrying Leah, thinking that he was given Rachel, the daughter he truly loved. Laban changed Jacob's wages several times when he worked for him. Jacob got fed up with his father-in-law's treatment and opportunistically ran away with his wives, children, and livestock, and headed back home. But he had a serious problem; his angry twin brother Esau: how would he face his avenger?

Jacob later returned to his self-willed scheming ways, once again, instead of trusting God. This despicable, self-serving man sent his wives and children ahead of him, watching to see how Esau would treat them. He put his wives and children in harm's way to save his own neck. How disgusting! Husbands are supposed to lay down their lives for wife and children, not to put themselves first. (How many times have we heard of a house on fire, and the first one out to safety is the man? Oh boy!)

God is able to do all things. We are not.

When Jacob had his second encounter with God, he was, once again, alone. God had him right where He wanted him. Jacob wrestled all night with this visitor from heaven. He refused to slacken his grasp unless the angel of The Lord blessed him. He got more than he bargained for, as the angel, prior to pronouncing a blessing, yanked Jacob's hip out of joint.

Jacob was now incapacitated and had no option but to trust God regarding his brother Esau. He couldn't run now. God miraculously softened Esau's heart and the twin brothers were gloriously reconciled.

Brothers and sisters, we must be convinced of five indisputable facts (which I learned from a message delivered by Chuck Swindoll):

1. God is able to do all things. We are not.
2. God's ways are perfect. Ours are not.
3. God sees the end from the beginning. We cannot.
4. God will have His way. We ought not.
5. God must get the glory. We should not.

With these attestations, our prayerful response should be, "Oh God, please take control of my life. I wholeheartedly surrender to You. Remove the sceptre (symbol of my will) out of my hands, and take it into Yours."

PENNY DIS

Takeaway(s) / New Idea(s)

___

___

___

___

___

Commitment(s)

___

___

___

___

___

Prayer / Thanksgiving / Resolution(s)

___

___

___

___

___

PENNY DIS

20

WHEN GOD SAYS "TIME'S UP"

I remember back in 1975, when sitting my GCE exams, we had an enigmatic chief invigilator who appeared to torment us with his time signals: "you will be happy to know that you have forty-five minutes left." We were sweating, and he was having the time of his life. When eventually, the time had elapsed, he declared almost triumphantly, "I am afraid that it is time to stoooopppp writing. Pens down, please." Our fate was now in the hands of the markers.

The story is told of a very hard-to-please employer, whose employees all hated his guts (and he had it a plenty).

PENNY DIS

The establishment's gardener had a striking resemblance to the despised boss, but the splendour of the employer's garb was in stark contrast to the gardener's rags. One day, we are told that the "grim reaper" came to the boss in his office with the fatal news, "Set your house in order. Your time is up. When I return tomorrow at noon, you will join the realm of the departed." The grim reaper immediately left, and the boss had an uneasy rest of the day and a sleepless night.

    When the boss arrived at work the next day, he sat at his desk contemplating his fate. The gardener was outside the office window doing his tasks for the day. The boss could not help but notice their resemblance. Suddenly, a brilliant idea flashed in his mind: change places with the gardener. The gardener was delighted with the exchange, which would only be for the day. The gardener could not believe his good fortune as he sat at the large well-polished desk. The boss, dressed in the gardener's rags, gave a sigh of relief. As promised, the angel of death returned at noon. "Your time is up," he reiterated. Come with me."

The man behind the desk was frightened out of his wits. He begged so earnestly for his life that the grim reaper felt sorry for him and reneged. "I can't leave empty-handed, however. I think I will take your gardener instead." When it's your time, there is no escape!

In 1 Kings 20, The Lord was gracious to wicked King Ahab, granting him victory over the, even more wicked, Syrian king Ben-Hadad. Instead of killing the Syrian monarch, as God required, Ahab set him free. A prophet of God revealed to Ahab that because he spared The Lord's enemy, he had forfeited his own life, and he had placed the nation of Israel in peril.

When it's your time, there is no escape!

Ahab later coveted his poor neighbour's vineyard. He offered to trade it for a larger vineyard or even purchase it at Naboth's price. Naboth declined both offers, to Ahab's great displeasure. Ahab threw an "adult tantrum" and refused to eat. When his wife Jezebel found out the reason for her husband's childish behaviour, she set about getting the vineyard for him herself. (She had, over the years, schooled Ahab in wickedness). She conspired with the elders to have Naboth killed, and then told her cowardly husband to go and take possession of the vineyard. As he did so, he was confronted by Elijah, who prophesied that dogs would lick up Ahab's blood in the same place that they had licked Naboth's blood. Ahab humbled himself, and God deferred his judgment.

Three years later, Ahab joined forces with Jehosophat, king of Judah, to fight against Ben-Hadad. Despite being warned that he would die in the battle, he chose to listen to false prophets who guaranteed victory. As he went to battle, he changed his kingly garments for those of an ordinary soldier, thinking if the war went badly for Israel, the Syrian army would pursue and kill Jehosophat, thinking that by his regal garments, he was Ahab. This is what almost happened. When the Syrians pursued Jehosophat, he cried out, and they recognized that he was not Ahab, and they stopped pursuing him. A Syrian archer accidentally fired his bow, and guess who the arrow fatally struck? You guessed correctly. Ahab was mortally wounded and died. Ahab's time was up.

One day, predetermined by Almighty God, your silver chord (and mine) will break. Time will be up. For me, that will be glorious (absent from the body, present with The Lord). What will it be for you (it is appointed unto men, once to die, but after this, the judgment) (Hebrews 9:27). Now is the accepted time, behold, today is the day of salvation. Come to Jesus while you may.
PENNY DIS

PENNY DIS

Takeaway(s) / New Idea(s)

_____

_____

_____

_____

_____

Commitment(s)

_____

_____

_____

_____

_____

Prayer / Thanksgiving / Resolution(s)

_____

_____

_____

_____

_____

21

GOD OF THE HILLS AND VALLEYS

In 1 Kings 20, despite Ahab's wickedness, God treated him with grace and mercy. The hills of Samaria were surrounded by the Syrian armies of king Ben-Hadad along with his confederation armies of thirty-two other kings. The situation was hopeless. Ben-Hadad threatened to take all of Israel's gold, silver, wives, children and even the goodliest. "All", he said, "is mine." Ahab was ready to concede without a fight, saying, "I am thine, and also all that I have." In arrogance, Ben-Hadad sent a message to king Ahab a second time, demanding that he personally hand over his gold, silver, wives and children. The elders advised Ahab not to hearken or consent to the Syrian king's demands, so war prevailed. God mercifully delivered Samaria, but Ahab did not credit God with the victory or change his wicked ways.

God is both God of the hills

and valleys.

An unnamed prophet of God came to Ahab after the victory, and cautioned him saying, 'Go, strengthen yourself, and mark, and see what thou doest (repent): for at the return of the year, Syria will again come up against thee' (1 Kings 20:22).

The servants of Ben-Hadad advised him (after his defeat) saying, "Their gods *are* gods of the hills; therefore they were stronger than we; but let us fight against them in the plain, and surely we shall be stronger than they" (1 Kings 20:23, KJV). Little did they know!

'And it came to pass that at the return of the year (as predicted), that Ben-Hadad numbered the Syrians and came against Israel in the valley of Aphek' (1 Kings 20:26). The same man of God came and spoke to Ahab saying, "Because the Syrians have said, The LORD *is* God of the hills, but he *is* not God of the valleys, therefore will I deliver all this great multitude into thine hand, and ye shall know that I *am* the LORD" (1 Kings 20:28, KJV). The battle ensued and God was true to His promise. Israel wrought a resounding second defeat over Ben-Hadad and his army, to make it known to all, that Israel's God is both God of the hills and valleys.

People of God, we do well to bear this in mind. We are encouraged by Job (and Brooklyn Tabernacle Choir) "in the good times (hills) praise His name: in the bad times (valleys) do the same. In everything, give the King of Kings all the thanks."

Easier said than done, isn't it? In our mountain-top experiences: when we pass that crucial exam, when we get married to the person of our dreams, when we hold our firstborn in our arms, when our team wins the championship, when our church purchases its first sanctuary, it is easy to acknowledge the God of the hills. But, when we fail that

critical exam, when our spouse walks away, when we lose the job we love, when we bury our favourite child, when we lose the championship, when our church building burns to the ground (all these, God forbid), can we still acknowledge the God of the valleys?
PENNY DIS

Takeaway(s) / New Idea(s)

_____

_____

_____

_____

_____

Commitment(s)

_____

_____

_____

_____

_____

Prayer / Thanksgiving / Resolution(s)

_____

_____

_____

_____

_____

PENNY DIS

22

PRIDE ASIDE

Pride goes before destruction and a haughty spirit before a fall (Proverbs 16:18). God resists the proud but gives grace to the humble (James 4:6). The vice of pride is sometimes referred to as the sin of sins. I have often wondered why, when there are murder, adultery and stealing. I have come to recognize, however, that this sin puts mortal man in the place of Almighty God.

Pride lurked in the garden of Eden. When the serpent tempted Eve, it was the fatal hook. The woman saw that the fruit was good for food (nothing wrong with that) and pleasant to the eyes (nothing wrong with that either) and was desired to make one wise (uh oh, problem!)... Satan lied when he promised, "Ye shall not surely die: For God doth know that in the day ye eat thereof, then your eyes shall be opened, and ye shall be as gods, knowing good and evil" (Genesis 3:5, KJV). Eve took the bait: took the fruit and ate, and gave also to her husband, and he ate also (Genesis 3:6). Man sought by this act of disobedience to be independent of God, charter of his own course, and master of his own destiny. What a disastrous miscalculation! Satan had instigated a second failed coup against God. You see, it was not his first attempt; he had done so millennia before. Lucifer was his original name and the beautiful cherub led the other angelic hosts in the worship of Almighty God. He was lifted in pride and coopted one-third of the angelic beings in a failed rebellion against God.

Read Isaiah 14:12 "How art thou fallen from heaven, O Lucifer, son of the morning! how art thou cut down to the ground, which didst weaken the nations!" (KJV). You see, Lucifer was the most beautiful of angels and was the worship leader for the praise of God (take heed worship leaders; it is so easy to lose focus and think it is about you). Not to us, O Lord, but to Thy name be glory, to Thy name be praise.

Pride goes before destruction
and a haughty spirit before a fall
(Proverbs 16:18).

The Lord said of Satan, "For thou hast said in thine heart, I will ascend into heaven, I will exalt my throne above the stars of God: I will sit also upon the mount of the congregation, in the sides of the north: I will ascend above the heights of the clouds; I will be like the most High" (Isaiah 14:13-14, KJV). What pomposity! Yet, thou shalt be cast down to hell, to the sides of the (bottomless) pit! When we are lifted in pride, we adopt the nature of its father, Lucifer, himself. Do you notice the proliferation of the words "I will" in the above words? "I" is a small word with devastating consequences. It seeks to magnify self above God. Ezekiel 28:12–19 tells us more about Lucifer's fall and condemnation:

'Thou select up the sum, full of wisdom and perfect in beauty...

Thou hast been in Eden, the garden of God; every precious stone was thy covering...

Thou art the anointed cherub that covered...

Thou wast upon the holy mountain of God...

Thou wast perfect in thy ways from the day thou wast created, till iniquity was found in thee ...

By the multitude of thy merchandise, they have filled the midst of thee with violence, and thou hast (greatly) sinned, therefore I (God) will cast thee as profane out of the mountains of God. I will destroy thee, O covering cherub.'

God certainly was not mincing words; He totally abhors pride and will ultimately judge it. Do you now understand why God literally fights against the proud in heart? It has its roots in genesis in Lucifer, and wherever this usurper raises its ugly head, God sets about crushing it.

When Israel (Achan) had committed the accursed thing after

Jericho's magnificent victory, and pridefully sent only a handful of soldiers to fight lowly Ai, God humbled them, causing them to flee before the enemy. God hates pride.

When Nebuchadnezzar exalted himself by saying, "Is not this great Babylon, that I have built...?" (Daniel 4:30, KJV). God banished him from his throne for seven years and afflicted him with insanity, causing him to become like a wild animal until he acknowledged that, "The most High ruleth in the kingdom of men" (Daniel 4:17, KJV). Many of today's rulers will suffer similar.

When the scribes and Pharisees looked down their noses at the Jewish populace, parading in glorious garments, pretending to be righteous, while having corrupt hearts and filthy hands, Jesus was at His fiercest as He "cut them down" and exposed them for the frauds that they were. Read the seven woes for the scribes and Pharisees, hypocrites, in Saint Matthew 23 (an entire chapter devoted to their condemnation). God hates pride, and moreover, when it comes from people who claim to be His representatives. Do you recognize the frequency with which false priests, pastors and bishops are being exposed by God, for the entire world to see the brute beasts, flesh seekers, power-mad minsters they truly are? Be not deceived, God is not mocked. If you, my reader, are a prideful imposter, He will soon expose you also. God hates pride. Be warned!

The apostle Paul, that great servant of God, saw and heard things and entered heavenly places, hearing words which he said were not lawful for man to utter. Read 2 Corinthians 12:1–6. With tremendous privilege comes tremendous responsibility. To guard Paul's heart from pride, as he put it, "Lest I should be exalted above measure," God gave him a thorn in his flesh, a messenger from Satan to buffet him constantly (2 Corinthians 12:7, KJV). We don't know exactly what this was, but some scholars believe it was vision problems. Paul prayed repeatedly for this infirmity to be taken from him, but God said (emphatically) "NO." HE gave Paul something far greater, HIS grace, which was more than sufficient to face the trial.

If you or I will dare to surrender our all and truly seek The Lord, we too will see wonderful things and enter heavenly places of privilege, while experiencing God's matchless power in our lives—with one caveat: all the glory belongs to Him. He still allows thorns in the flesh, messengers of Satan, to buffet and keep God's servants humble. So, that very critical spouse, that wayward child, that ungrateful congregation, that overbearing boss, that neighbour that gets on your nerves and that sickness that will not go away, may just be from God to keep your head out of the clouds and keep you on your knees. Don't get mad or frustrated. When the circumstances of life knock you off your feet, simply kneel and pray.

PENNY DIS

PENNY DIS

Takeaway(s) / New Idea(s)

_____

_____

_____

_____

_____

Commitment(s)

_____

_____

_____

_____

_____

Prayer / Thanksgiving / Resolution(s)

_____

_____

_____

_____

_____

23

THE PURSUIT OF HAPPINESS

Godless pursuits of pleasure in this life will never satisfy. It is said concerning this generation, that never before have so many had so much, yet remain so dissatisfied. A century ago, the list of things necessary for a person to be satisfied would fill a few lines. Today, that list could fill volumes. It is not just as simple as, "Don't worry. Be happy."

Solomon was the wisest man (Jesus apart), and yet in his later years, he was an unhappy and unfulfilled man. He allowed his insatiable appetite for ungodly women (300 wives and 700 concubines) to turn his heart from God, and his life spiralled downward into darkness and misery. Come along with me and get a sneak peek into Solomon's vain and frustrating pursuit, found in the book of Ecclesiastes.

First, Solomon tried pleasure. "I said to myself, 'Come now, I will make a test of pleasure; enjoy yourself.' But again, this also was vanity" (Ecclesiastes 2:1, NRSV). Pleasure did not do the trick for Solomon and it will not work for you, my dear reader. We live in an extremely pleasure-seeking world today. There are sports, entertainment, arts, travel, and the like. These involve trillions of dollars spent on them annually, yet dissatisfaction grows. How many have found the pleasureful exploits of the Christmas season had evaporated, and it was only in the first week of the new year? Our "satisfaction needle" is still on empty. The Carnivals, the parties, the movies, the sex, the drugs, the social media, you name it, all have failed to bring lasting satisfaction. They promise so much yet deliver so little. "What next?" we ask. "What deception?" we are really asking, and we keep falling for it.

Solomon tried laughter (comedy), and this did not work either. You can laugh your troubles away, some foolishly believe. Comedy has devolved from silent to unspeakable. We make fun out of homosexuality, debauchery, drunkenness and adultery. We laugh at things God hates. Fools make a mockery of sin, but righteousness exalts while sin brings reproach. When we have had our last laugh and are alone with our thoughts and our miserable life, do not hot tears drench our pillows? Solomon, you are absolutely correct; laughter is madness.

Godless pursuits of pleasure in this life will never satisfy.

    Solomon tried to find satisfaction in strong drink. If he had today's drugs, he would have tried those, too. How many contemporary idols are going or have gone this route, even to their death: Michael Jackson, Prince, Whitney Houston, just to name a few? Who will be next. You?

    Solomon tried wisdom. Yesterday's version of today's education and the endless degrees. The Bible says that one of the last-day indicators is people ever-learning but never coming to a knowledge of the truth. The Bible also says the fear of The Lord is the beginning of wisdom and the knowledge of The Holy One is understanding. Men (and women) professing themselves to be wise become as fools, saying there is no God. The biggest fools of all have academic letters behind their names. Simply look at the moral mess of their lives and how sadly they end. Hear some final words of hopelessness and despair.

Solomon tried wealth, real estate, music, women, accomplishments and accolades, Whatever his eyes desired, he did not keep them from. Yes, Solomon tried it all, and to what end? In Ecclesiastes 2:17 Solomon declares, "So I hated life, because what is done under the sun was grievous to me; for all is vanity and a chasing after wind" (NRSV). Solomon was on the verge of committing suicide. Do you recognize the increasing number of, even wealthy, people who are turning to suicide today? What deception? Do you not understand that death is not the end? Jesus Christ will be the final judge, and eternal hell awaits all Christ rejectors.

Does it make sense to face hell on earth only to face eternal hell? But there is hope. Solomon came to a godly conclusion after his godless pursuit. Ecclesiastes 12:1 states, "Remember your creator in the days of your youth, before the days of trouble come..." (NRSV). Seek and serve The Lord while you are young. Don't waste your youth. Young people, please take heed. Ecclesiastes 12:13–14 says, "Let us hear the conclusion of the whole matter: Fear God, and keep his commandments: for this is the whole duty of man. For God shall bring every work into judgment, with every secret thing, whether it be good, or whether it be evil" (KJV). God created you to worship Him, and until we do, nothing else will satisfy our thirsty soul. I close with a thought from a childhood chorus by Ira Stanphill: "Happiness is The Lord," through knowing and experiencing The Saviour (his favour), and through a change in behaviour for Him.

PENNY DIS

PENNY DIS

Takeaway(s) / New Idea(s)

_____

_____

_____

_____

_____

Commitment(s)

_____

_____

_____

_____

_____

Prayer / Thanksgiving / Resolution(s)

_____

_____

_____

_____

_____

24

GOOD LOOKS

When I was a child, hearing that Grandma (my father's mother) was coming to visit filled me and my siblings with great dread. She came to run things (boy, she had us running) and dished out orders like "bakra master" himself. Resistance was futile. She assigned (mandated) every conceivable chore with great liberalism. At times, my face revealed my displeasure. She would sometimes respond, "Bwoy, yu tink yu is here only fi yu guud looks (boy, do you think you are here only for your good looks)?" She made me understand, in no uncertain terms, that I had a vital role to play in the smooth running of our household. She also acknowledged the great fact that yours truly was good-looking. I challenge everyone (including myself) to pause and take some "good looks" at the precious day called "today."

First, LOOK UPWARD. See God in all His fullness. See Him in His magnificent creation. "The heavens declare the glory of God; and the firmament showeth His handiwork" (Psalm 19:1, KJV). Let the universe fill you with awe and wonder. Let the vast oceans, rivers, cascading waterfalls, majestic sunrises, and sunsets, diverse forests, teeming with wondrous wildlife, cause you to lavish Him with total praise. Then consider mankind in its variety of languages and hues, all created in His image and likeness. Let this take your breath away. Then get personal and, like the psalmist, praise God, for you are fearfully and wonderfully made.

I know that many are dissatisfied with their bodies, and many resolve to exercise. Gym memberships increase in January, only to be broken before February. By all means, do what you can, but recognize that you are more than a body. Don't fall for the misguided notion that the physical is all; you have a beautiful mind, soul, and spirit that needs to be nurtured also.

See God in Jesus, who came to reveal the Father to us. See God in the great gift of His baby boy, but don't stop at the cradle. Go all the way to the cross of Calvary. There again ponder the gravity of your sin (and mine) and God's unconditional love for us. Remember, God, without man, is still God. But man, without God, is woefully lost and inadequate. If you desire to know your worth, get to know your Creator, and worship Him continually and passionately.

Second, LOOK BACKWARDS. It is sometimes said that we see the hand of God in the rearview mirror. God's ways are past finding out, and in the present moment, can be misunderstood or even maligned. Remember the psalmist that almost backslid because he couldn't understand that God allowed the wicked to prosper and the righteous to suffer? It was only when he went into God's presence and saw things from God's perspective that he understood. As tough as last year was, God saw you through it. Give Him praise.

If you desire to know your worth, get to know your Creator, and worship Him continually and passionately.

Third, LOOK FORWARD. "The just shall live by his faith" (Habakkuk 2:4, NKJV). This year or next could very well be your breakthrough year, your year of Jubilee. That job, that promotion, that proposal/marriage, that baby, that scholarship, that pastorship, that ministry opportunity, that healing, that missions trip, that house or final mortgage payment, that prodigal's return, fill in the blank... YES, this could be the time. Keep trusting God and give Him your all. In all that you do, however, love Him far more than these gifts that you desire of Him. What about The Lord's promised return? Is heaven on your mind? There is a hymn that comes to mind, which begins like this:

It May Be Morn
"It may be at morn when the day is awaking,

When sunlight through darkness and shadow is breaking,
That Jesus will come in the fullness of glory
To receive from the world His own."
H. L. Turner

Oh, Lord Jesus, how long?

Four, LOOK INWARD. How have you changed since last year? For the better or for the worse? Are there things God wants to change or remove, but you have been resistant or even defiant? Do you more resemble your Saviour? Do others see Jesus in you? Remember, Christlikeness is our ultimate eternal destiny. Take stock of your life. What needs to go must go so that what needs to grow, can grow. "Only one life, 'twill soon be past; only what's done for Christ will last" (C. T. Studd).

Five, LOOK AROUND. A hurting world of humanity stands at your doorstep. They need YOU: your godly lifestyle, your unconditional love, your genuine embrace, and your unique input in their lives. Let heaven be vastly populated by people who will, on that great day, say, "Thank you for giving to The Lord; I'm a life that was changed by

PENNY DIS

not just your money, but also your time, talents and your infectious love."
PENNY DIS

Takeaway(s) / New Idea(s)

_____

_____

_____

_____

_____

Commitment(s)

_____

_____

_____

_____

_____

Prayer / Thanksgiving / Resolution(s)

_____

_____

_____

_____

_____

PENNY DIS

25

BUT FOR THE GRACE OF GOD

The closer we walk with God, two realities become abundantly clear: God's infinite holiness, and our wretched sinfulness. We fail to fully understand the latter because we do not fathom what sin is, and how sin (no matter how small or insignificant in our eyes) offends God. Let us reflect on some verses of scripture that relate to sin:

1. "For all have sinned and come short of the glory of God" (Romans 3:23, NKJV). Everything that falls short of divine perfection is sin. Oops!!!
2. Sin is the transgression of the law (1 John 3:4). James informs us that "breaking one of God's Holy

commandments, makes us guilty of violating all ten. The law is there to convince us of our sinfulness. Can you see how futile it is to hinge your salvation to the keeping of the law? Only Jesus Christ kept the law perfectly.

3. That which is not of faith is sin (Romans 14:23). Anything that is motivated or originates from self-effort is tainted with sin.
4. "Therefore to him that knoweth to do good, and doeth *it* not, to him it is sin" (James 4:17, KJV). We sin by omission far more often than by commission.
5. "The thought of foolishness is sin" (Proverbs 24:9, ASV). Wow! I've been sinning big time! Have you?

Do you (and I) see more clearly what great sinners we all are? We are devoid of righteousness, except for the imputed righteousness of Christ, that the Father gives to those who believe on HIS SON. When next we see an abhorrent sinner, remember, "There go I, but for the grace of God."

Let us consider the life of the great apostle Paul (the apostle born out of due time) (1 Corinthians 15:8). It is instructive how he viewed himself as he matured in his knowledge of Christ. Early in his Christian experience, Paul referred to himself as having laboured more abundantly than all the other apostles (1 Corinthians 5:10). He also perceived himself to have come behind none of the other apostles (2 Corinthians 11:5). Later on, he referred to himself as being the least of the apostles (1 Corinthians 15: 9). Then again, he said he was less than the least of all the saints (Ephesians 3: 8). Finally, he referred to himself as being the chief of sinners (1 Timothy 1:15).

When next pride rears its ugly head in our lives, let us think of our lovely Lord.

Look at the condescension (in first-person view), from the chief of the apostles to the chief of sinners. It begs the question, if one who we highly esteem could eventually think so lowly if himself, then what is the basis of our pride? The scriptures admonish you not to "think of yourself more highly than you ought" (Romans 12:3, NIV). Also, you are to " Mind not high things, but condescend to men of low estate. Be not wise in your own conceits." (Romans 12:16, KJV).

When next pride rears its ugly head in our lives, let us think of our lovely Lord. "For you know the generous act of our Lord Jesus Christ, that though he was rich, yet for your sakes he became poor, so that by his poverty you might become rich." (2 Corinthians 8:9, NRSV). Read again Philippians 2:6–8 and take careful note of the degree of the condescension of Jesus' humiliation, "Who, being in the form of God, thought it not robbery to be equal with God: But made himself of no reputation, and took upon him the form of a servant, and was made in the likeness of men: And being found in fashion as a man, he humbled himself, and became obedient unto death, even the death of the cross" (KJV). HALLELUJAH! What a SAVIOUR!!! The greatness inside you is there by GRACE: His Grace.
PENNY DIS

Takeaway(s) / New Idea(s)

_____

_____

_____

_____

_____

Commitment(s)

_____

_____

_____

_____

_____

Prayer / Thanksgiving / Resolution(s)

_____

_____

_____

_____

_____

PENNY DIS

26

OH FREEDOM!

Saint John 8:32 and verse 36 say, "And ye shall know the truth, and the truth shall make you free... If the Son therefore shall make you free, ye shall be free indeed" (KJV). We are no longer slaves to fear. We are children of God. Many sons and daughters of Africa have known the harsh realities of slavery and its residual repercussions. One person has rightly said "slavery has not really been abolished, it has simply become more covertly sophisticated." The children of Israel have also known the bitterness of slavery, having been mercilessly enslaved for over 400 years in Egypt.

For a period, Joseph (11th son of Jacob) had been a celebrity of sorts in Egypt after interpreting Pharaoh's dreams. His reward was promotion to the second highest position of power in the land. He not only delivered Egypt from famine, but also saved his family from starvation. He too had been given prophetic dreams from God regarding his destiny, which he shared with his brothers—big mistake—and his father (Genesis 37:5–11).

Dream 1: 'We were binding sheaves of grain out in The field, when suddenly my sheaf rose and stood upright, while yours (his brothers') gathered around mine and bowed down to it.' His brothers, who already hated him, were not amused (Genesis 37:7–8).

Dream 2: "The sun and moon and eleven stars were bowing down to me" (Genesis 37:9, NIV). Daddy and mummy also?! Now daddy Jacob was not amused. *Me, bow down to my son?* However, unlike the brothers, his father kept the matter in mind (like Mary the mother of Jesus kept the sayings concerning her Son and pondered them in her heart) (Genesis 37:9–11).

Problems started brewing for the Israelites after the death of Joseph and his generation. In Exodus 1:7, we read, 'But the Israelites were fruitful and multiplied (God's original mandate of Genesis 1:28) greatly, and became exceedingly numerous, so the land was filled with them.'

The Lord knows how to deliver the righteous.

They had overstayed their welcome, now posing a threat to their hosts. Verse 8 states, that then a new king, who knew not Joseph, came to power in Egypt, and the rest, they say, is history; over 400 years of slavery ensued. But wait, where did we previously hear of a 400-year enslavement of Abram's descendants? Oh, yes, Genesis 15:13–14. The Bible says, 'Know for certain that your [Abram's] descendants will be strangers in a country not your own, and they will be enslaved and mistreated four hundred years. But I will punish the nation they serve as slaves, and afterward they will come out with great possessions.' Promise made, promise kept.

There was a late twist to the freedom saga; Pharaoh had a change of heart after letting the Israelites go. *What have we done?* he thought, "We have let the Israelites go, and have lost their services. Services!?" A strange way if depicting forced enslavement of a people... The scriptures tell us that The Lord hardened Pharaoh's heart, so he pursued the Israelites, seeking to recapture them. But God had a plan, hallelujah! The Lord knows how to deliver the righteous. After the Red Sea miraculously parted, allowing the Israelites to pass on dry ground, the Egyptian army assayed to do likewise. When they were halfway, God caused the waters of the Red Sea to return, drowning the entire Egyptian army. In "Redemption Song", Robert Nester Marley (Bob Marley) sings about "these songs of freedom..." Well, let me introduce you to a greater freedom song, the song of Moses and Miriam in Exodus 15:1–18. Verse 11 poses the question, "Who *is* like unto Thee, oh Lord among gods?... fearful *in* praises, doing wonders?" (KJV). A rhetorical ask, if ever there was one, for there is none to compare to The God of Abraham, Isaac and Jacob. Read Isaiah 49:12–26.

There is, however, a more deadly form of slavery than physical enslavement, slavery to sin, and we are all subject to it. Again, Romans 3:23 states, "For all have sinned, and come short of the glory of God" (KJV). Romans 5:12 further explains, 'Wherefore as by one man (Adam) sin entered the world, and death because of sin, so therefore death has been passed unto all men, in that all have sinned.' Not only are all sinners, but all are enslaved and sold to sin. Jesus said in Saint John 8:34, 'Truly, truly I say unto you, whoever commits sin is a slave of sin.' The apostle Paul reiterates this in Romans 6:16, explaining that when you offer yourself to someone to obey them as a slave, you are a slave to the one you obey–whether you are a slave to sin, which leads to death or otherwise?" Chapter 6:20 states, 'When you were slaves to sin, you were free from the control of righteousness (sinfully out of control).' The only freedom the unregenerate sinner knows is the freedom of choice of sins he or she commits. And you and I thought we were free!

The only ones on the planet Earth or in heaven who are truly free have acknowledged that "nothing in my hands I bring; simply to Thy cross I cling" (Rock of Ages) or "just as I am without one plea, but that Thy blood was shed for me. And as Thou bidst me come to Thee, o Lamb of God, I come. I come (Just As I Am). Have you, my dear reader, been freed from sin's bondage and power in your life? Today Jesus is tenderly calling you. Charles Wesley, in his great hymn expressing his conversion, wrote:

And Can It Be?
"Long my imprisoned spirit lay,
Fast bound in sin and nature's night.
Thine eye diffused a quickening ray.
I woke, the dungeon flamed with light.
My chains fell off, my heart was free.
I rose, went forth, and followed Thee."

That's why Jesus Christ was crucified. "The Spirit of the Lord is on me, because he has anointed me... to proclaim freedom for the prisoners" (Saint Luke

4:18, NIV). For if the Son shall make you free, you shall be truly free.
PENNY DIS

PENNY DIS

Takeaway(s) / New Idea(s)

_____

_____

_____

_____

_____

Commitment(s)

_____

_____

_____

_____

_____

Prayer / Thanksgiving / Resolution(s)

_____

_____

_____

_____

_____

27

LIFE UNLIMITED

The words of The Lord say, 'I am come, that they (you) might have life, and have it more abundantly' (Saint John 10:10). I remember as a youth growing up in Jamaica, a singer named Ernie Smith (a celebrity of sorts, who lived down the street from me) was featured in an advertisement, singing one of his signature tunes "Life is Just for Living." As he held and sipped from a bottle of Red Stripe bear, he changed the words for "I'd rather have a Red Stripe." I suppose the message of the advertisement was, "Red Stripe is what living is all about." Really!?

The man accredited with being the wisest ever (King Solomon), turned away from the God of his father, and turned to things and people to find purpose and meaning in life. In respect to marital relationships, he was, by far, more than his father's son. King David was accredited with about seven wives (I've lost count). Solomon had 300 wives and 700 concubines. A thousand women! *Are you kidding me?!* you ask. No, I am not kidding.

Solomon either never read or chose to ignore Deuteronomy 17. Verse 17 is quite poignant, speaking of the ruler (king) over God's people: "Neither shall he multiply wives to himself, that his heart turn not away: neither shall he greatly multiply to himself silver and gold" (KJV). Verse 16 says, "But he shall not multiply horses to himself, nor cause the people to return to Egypt, to the end that he should multiply horses: forasmuch as the LORD hath said unto you, 'Ye shall henceforth return no more that way...'" (KJV). Solomon failed on all counts. I suppose the chip does not fall far from the block.

This was not always the case with Solomon. Early in his reign, we read in

1Kings 3:3, 'And Solomon loved the Lord; walking in the statutes of his father David (but not completely), except that he sacrificed and burned incense at the high places (idolatry in violation of the second commandment).' Did Solomon not know that you cannot fellowship at the altar of God and also fellowship at the altar of demons?

Where did Solomon learn idolatry? 1 Kings 3:1 says, "Solomon made affinity with Pharaoh of Egypt..." (KJV). *What?! After Egypt used your people as slaves for 400 years? Solomon, how could you?* Solomon's slippery slide into apostasy continued. In 1 Kings 11:1, we read, "But king Solomon loved many strange women, together with the daughter of Pharaoh" (KJV). Uh oh! This is unbelievable! What is it with men of God and "strange" women? Samson and Delilah the Philistine, David and Uriah's wife Bathsheba, and now Solomon and the daughter of the Egyptian Pharaoh... And what of the other 999 (not the ninety and nine).

Another advertisement of my youth depicted a rich sheik seeking beds at a furniture store. One king and forty-nine queens. He ordered, much to the amazement of the salesman. Then the cameras switched to his giggling harem of forty-nine wives. Solomon made this sheik look like he wasn't even trying!

1 Kings 11:4 and verse 6 gives this sad, but to be expected commentary, 'For it was so, when Solomon was old, that his wives turned his heart from God... And Solomon did evil in the sight of the Lord...' He had it all, as one would say, but ended up a loser.

Why are so many still sharing in Solomon's failed search for pleasure and purpose apart from God? Think of Prince, Michael Jackson, Liberace, Whitney Houston, et al. Why won't we learn as well that the God-sized hole in our hearts can only been filled by God? 'For what is a man profited if he (or she) should gain the whole world and lose his soul? Or what will a man give in exchange for his soul?' (Saint Matthew 16:26).

Saint Mark 10:17–22 tells of a wealthy, young ruler of the Jews who came with (false) urgency and humility to Jesus, seeking the gift of eternal life. After some small talk, Jesus "cut to the chase." 'Go, sell all that you have, give it to the poor, and you will have (greater) riches in heaven; and come, follow me.' The scriptures say, in response to Jesus' command, 'He was sad at these words (of Jesus), and went away sorrowful, for he had great possessions.' This man could have been made an Elder in many an Evangelical Church, but Jesus disqualified him for the kingdom of heaven.

Why are so many still sharing in Solomon's failed search for pleasure and purpose apart from God?

You see, he who thought he had kept all ten of the commandments perfectly from his youth had been guilty of breaking the first and greatest along with the second: No other God, and no idols. As such, he was guilty of breaking all ten according to James 2:10. So much for the modern-day Sabbath-keepers (so they think) and law breakers who seek salvation by their good works, many of whom think they are the only ones going to heaven!

Contrast this wealthy, upright (seemingly), Jewish young man, with another wealthy, scoundrel Jew who was not so young, named Zaccheus. Remember him, Shorty? He had gained his immense wealth by extortion of his own people for the Roman oppressors, taking the extras for his own coffers. He was despicable, dishonest, despised, and desolate. (I just love alliteration.) Because of his vertical challenge, he climbed a sycamore tree (the only one with limbs low enough for him to climb) to get a curious glimpse of Jesus. When Jesus looked up and saw him, He said to him, 'Zaccheus, (HE knew him by name, just as HE knows you, my reader, by name) make haste and come down, for I must stay at your house (today).' *You know me? You want to come to my house?!* I don't know whether Zaccheus climbed down or fell down (I will ask him when I get to heaven), but he got down quickly to meet the first Jew who had anything kind to say to him in life. Indeed, salvation came to that son of Abraham that day, a full dose of it.

With salvation and eternal life come real joy, not in things, but in a relationship with Jesus Christ of Nazareth.

The first rich man clutched his wealth and walked away from Jesus, sorrowful. But the second man delighted in giving his wealth away, having found an externally greater treasure, Jesus Christ Himself.

Do you own this Saviour and, with Him, eternal life? Or do you believe the lie that "Red Stripe, et al." is what life is all about? Stop your pitiful existence of substandard living, and in Jesus find the life unlimited that HE graciously offers.
PENNY DIS

PENNY DIS

Takeaway(s) / New Idea(s)

_____

_____

_____

_____

_____

Commitment(s)

_____

_____

_____

_____

_____

Prayer / Thanksgiving / Resolution(s)

_____

_____

_____

_____

_____

28

PROMISES, PROMISES

The story is told of a scorpion that needed to get across a river. He asked a frog to give him a ride over to the other side on his back. The frog was quite apprehensive to do so because he knew how lethal the scorpion's sting was. He shared the reason for his hesitancy with the scorpion. The scorpion "crossed his heart and hoped to die" that he would not sting the frog. The frog took him at his word and complied. Mid-stream, the scorpion reneged on his promise and fatally stung the frog, much to the amphibian's dismay. As they both sank to their watery grave, the frog asked the scorpion why he would do such a thing.

The scorpion replied, "It is my nature, and I could not resist."

Let us consider the number of our own broken promises to God.

I spent two years living on the campus of The Mico Teachers' College. During the week of orientation, every "grub" had to memorize the college pledge, "I promise, on my honour, that I will obey ALL College rules..." We could be accosted by any senior student and be required to say the pledge, to which we had to stand at attention, raise our right hand, and recite, word-perfect, the college pledge. After the orientation week was passed, it didn't take some first-year students long to break every one of the rules they had faithfully promised to uphold.

Israel was no stranger to breaking promises that they made to God. When they came to the wilderness of Sinai, Moses went up the mountain to meet with God. In Exodus 19, The Lord said to Moses, 'Tell the children of Israel: ye have seen what I did to the Egyptians, and how I bore you on eagle's wings, and brought you to Myself. Now therefore, if you will indeed obey My voice, and keep My covenant, then you shall be a special treasure (above all people) to Me, for all the earth is Mine, and you shall be to Me, a kingdom of priests, and a holy nation.' After Moses relayed God's message to the people, they solemnly promised 'all that The Lord has spoken, we will do.' Moses then offered a sacrifice to God and splashed the blood of the slain oxen on the people, sealing the covenant with blood. They had lied. About forty days later, they were worshipping the golden calf, led by Moses' people-pleasing brother and high priest Aaron. Then the people rose up early on the next day, offered burnt offerings, and brought peace offerings, and the people sat down to eat and rose to carousel (the first carnival). Promise made, promise broken.

Again, under the leadership of Joshua, we read in Joshua 24:24 (after he had challenged to serve The Lord wholeheartedly), it was said, 'We will worship God. What He says, we will do.' Once again, they lied. Soon they were in the promised land, worshipping the

Canaanite false gods, taking the ungodly women as wives for their sons, and giving their daughters in marriage to ungodly men. Promises. No wonder God berated His people in Isaiah 1, 'Bring Me no more futile sacrifices... your New Moons and your appointed feasts, My soul hates... When you spread your hands, I will hide My face from you... even though you pray many prayers, I will not listen.'

Before you and I are harshly critical of Israel for their broken promises, let us consider the number of our own broken promises to God. "Oh God, if only You would get me out if this problem, I will serve You." So, God delivered you, and have you kept your word? NO! Or "God, if you give me a husband, I will serve you faithfully." So, God gives you a husband, and are you serving Him faithfully? NO!!! Do we truly understand who God is? My brothers and sisters, let us pay our vows. God is faithful, and so should we be.
PENNY DIS

Takeaway(s) / New Idea(s)

_____

_____

_____

_____

_____

Commitment(s)

_____

_____

_____

_____

_____

Prayer / Thanksgiving / Resolution(s)

_____

_____

_____

_____

_____

PENNY DIS

29

HOLY FOREVER

When did holiness become a bad word for the people of God? "She or he is too holy" is many times the indictment for a Christian who is simply passionate for God. Many times, the greatest fight an aspiring Christian in pursuit of God can get may not come from unbelievers, but from people who profess Christ.

I remember vividly, a young mid-teen in my Sunday School (in my birth country of Jamaica) who trusted Christ as Lord of her life. She chose to honour God by wearing a head covering to Sunday School as well as church meetings. The sweet soul was mercilessly ridiculed by her peers and unkind comments were made by older Christians. I am not sure where she is today, but the last I remember, she was not walking with The Lord anymore.

Do you recall the response of even some of Jesus' disciples when Mary poured the ointment from her broken alabaster box, and lavished it on Jesus? She washed The Master's feet with her tears, kissed them, and dried them with her hair. It was an awkward moment for all the onlookers, as they had never seen or personally expressed that kind of selfish abandonment in worship. "Why this waste?" the soon-to-be traitor (Judas) expressed in disgust (Saint Matthew 26:8, NIV). 'This perfume could have sold, and the proceeds use to feed the poor' (Saint Matthew 26:8). Jesus rebuked the critics, saying, 'Leave her alone... She is preparing my body for my upcoming burial' (Saint Mark 14:6). This worshipper perceived in the Spirit something the tough-headed disciples didn't, even though Jesus had repeatedly told them of His impending death.

I was once one who felt uncomfortable in the presence of demonstrable, holy, lavish praise of

Jesus. When worshippers raised their hands, or fell to their knees, there was personal unease on my part. But didn't I do seemingly out-of-the-box and, sometimes, silly things for my wife when we were dating to express my love for her? Then why did I have inhibition when expressing my love for Jesus? After all the Saviour did for me. I simply was too self-conscious, not wanting to be labelled as a holy fanatic. Shame on me!

    I recall hearing of a Christian man who wore one of these sandwich advertisements. On the front stated, "I am a fool for Jesus", which evoked public ridicule. The voices however fell silent when persons saw the message on the back, "Whose fool are you?" Reminds me of a blast from the past, the song "Everybody's Somebody's Fool." I'd rather be Jesus' fool, wouldn't you?

    So, why is holiness not celebrated by the church of Jesus Christ, in manner, speech and even attire? Exodus 28:36 tells us that a part of the priestly garb was a plate of gold, which had engraved on it "Holiness to the Lord" (KJV).

    1 Chronicles 16:29 says, "Worship the LORD in the beauty of holiness" (NKJV). God lamented Israel's

backsliding in Jeremiah 2. He said, "I remember you, The kindness of your youth, the love of your betrothal, when you went after Me in the wilderness, in a land not sown. Israel was holiness to the Lord" (Jeremiah 2:2–3, NKJV). I sense God's heartbreak. Like the church at Ephesus in Revelation 2, Israel, and many times ourselves, have left our first love. Donnie McClurkin expressed God's feelings in his song "So In Love." In the lyrics of the song, God asks what He did to you to be treated the way He is by you when all He did was to try to prove to you He loved you. Can you sense God's tears?

Everybody's Somebody's Fool.

Haven't we been entreated in Leviticus 19:20 to be holy, for The Lord is holy? And weren't we warned in Hebrews 12:14 that without holiness, none will see The Lord? And aren't we encouraged in 2 Corinthians 7:1, to perfect in holiness in the fear of The Lord, and in Hebrews 12:10, to be partakers of His holiness? And aren't we admonished

in 1 Timothy 2:15 to continue in faith and holiness? Mount Zion children, walk holy. You must live it. Then, and only then, can you sing it.
PENNY DIS

PENNY DIS

Takeaway(s) / New Idea(s)

_____

_____

_____

_____

_____

Commitment(s)

_____

_____

_____

_____

_____

Prayer / Thanksgiving / Resolution(s)

_____

_____

_____

_____

_____

30

BE REAL

There are few things as appealing as authenticity, and there are even fewer things more repugnant than hypocrisy. A good-old song has as its title "Ain't Nothing Like the Real Thing." When people are two-faced (this is the root meaning of a hypocrite), one may be tempted to ask, "Will the real "mister" please stand up?"

Merchants of pottery, in a past era, would proclaim that their wares were "sincere," which meant without wax. Charlatans would conceal the flaws in their clay vessels with wax (similar to what women, and some men, do with cosmetics). To prove the genuineness of the article, one needed only to place it for a while in the sun or in an oven. If wax was used, it would melt, and the flaws would be obvious.

If there is one thing Jesus hates, it is religious hypocrisy. He was scathing in His criticism of the scribes and Pharisees. In Saint Matthew 23, He laid it on thick as He exposed them for the frauds they were. Read it for yourself. Six times, He said to them, 'Woe to you teachers of the law and Pharisees... HYPOCRITES!' Once, He referred to them as blind guides (and we know, if the blind lead the blind, both will tumble into a ditch). The way Jesus gave it to them is evidence of His hatred for pretence.

> If there is one thing
> Jesus hates,
> it is religious hypocrisy.

In Saint Matthew 19:13–15, mothers of a town named Salem brought their children to Jesus for Him to bless them. As far as the insensitive disciples were concerned, Jesus had "bigger fish to fry." The Bible says the disciples sternly rebuked these mothers and turned them and their little darlings away. Jesus was incensed, and He said, "Let the little children come to me, and do not hinder them, for the kingdom of heaven belongs to such as these" (Saint Matthew19:14, NIV). Then He placed His hands on them and blessed them.

Several times in the scriptures, Jesus used children as object lessons to His "tough-headed" disciples. In Saint Matthew 18, the disciples were arguing concerning which of them was the greatest. To teach them a lesson, Jesus placed a child in their midst. What is it about children that is important to emulate? I guess it is their innocence, transparency, trusting nature, and their unpretentiousness. Jesus said to His disciples, "Verily I say unto you, Except ye be converted, and become as little children, ye shall not enter into the kingdom of heaven" (Saint Matthew 18:3, KJV).

So, my friend, will we stop our pretence, self-righteousness and hypocrisy? Remember, all things are bare before Him. You can't bandulu Jesus! If we are to find acceptance by

PENNY DIS

Him, we must come to Him as we truly are. Let's get real with the real God.
PENNY DIS

Takeaway(s) / New Idea(s)

_____

_____

_____

_____

_____

Commitment(s)

_____

_____

_____

_____

_____

Prayer / Thanksgiving / Resolution(s)

_____

_____

_____

_____

_____

PENNY DIS

31

THE POTTER'S HAND

Through all the vicissitudes of my life, there has been one constant, the grace, mercy and faithfulness of God. HE has been with me and for me all the time.

Of all my siblings, I was the only one who was born at home. I am the second born to my mother, and Miss Ruby's first son. We were so close. My father jokingly disowned me at birth. He could never have a child that was so ugly; that is what my mother told me he responded at his first look at me. As I grew, there was no doubt in anyone's mind who my father was, so either I was not as ugly as he said, or he was not as good looking as he thought. At age twenty, my life was pointless, directionless, and useless. I had flunked out of university twice and was heading nowhere in a hurry. Two significant persons changed the course of my life; Jesus Christ and, about ten years later, my beloved wife and best friend Sandra Marie. Both have been working on me ever since, to varying degrees of success. I am like clay in the hands of the Master Potter Himself.

Without the potter,

the clay is without form and void.

In Jeremiah 18, God commanded the prophet to go to the potter's house, where he was to learn a symbolic and important lesson. Jeremiah obeyed and closely observed the potter at work. There is nothing quite like watching a master at his or her craft. There he was fashioning the clay on the spinning wheel, when suddenly he sensed a flaw in the vessel. He did not patch it up, but rather smashed it, wet it, put it back on the wheel, and refashioned it to

perfection. Jeremiah learned a great lesson that day, one that I am slowly learning even after 64 years. God is the potter; we are the clay. Without the potter, the clay is without form and void. The potter has a perfect image in mind for the seemingly insignificant blob, and the clay does not have a clue of its potential. But why does the potter smash the unfinished vessel when he senses the flaw? You see, God does not patch up brokenness, He recreates. Therefore, if any man be in Christ Jesus, he is a new creation... the old is gone, the new is come. When God sees anything in His children that does not resemble His Son Jesus, He breaks us and then lovingly restores us. This process is quite painful, but the rewards are incomparable. Is God taking you through this painful process right now? Be patient under the mighty hand of God and make patience have its perfect work in you: Christlikeness will be the result. Mold me, guide me, lead me, walk beside me, I give my life to the Potter's hand. This is my prayer. Will you make it yours today?
PENNY DIS

PENNY DIS

Takeaway(s) / New Idea(s)

_____

_____

_____

_____

_____

Commitment(s)

_____

_____

_____

_____

_____

Prayer / Thanksgiving / Resolution(s)

_____

_____

_____

_____

_____

32

THAT'S THE THING ABOUT PRAISE

Jericho walls were shut up tight. Man, those walls were high and broad—impregnable; victory seemed impossible. The strategy declared by General Joshua would have seemed ridiculous, to say the least, but he said that was what God said. With trumpeters and the choir leading the way, the army was to march around Jericho once a day for six days, then seven times on the seventh day. They were to blow the trumpets and shout the praises of JEHOVAH.

What a laugh the soldiers on the wall must have had, as those silly

Israelites marched around for six days, then for six times on the seventh. Subsequently, the trumpets blew, and the people shouted a mighty shout of praise to JEHOVAH, and Jericho's mighty walls fell. Praise accomplishes wonders. That's the thing about praise!

The backs of Paul and Silas were bloody and sore. They had been severely beaten and they were chained in an awful dungeon. Their crime? It was delivering a slave damsel possessed with a spirit of divination. This resulted in the loss of her powers of divination. Her owner was not amused! At about the midnight hour, instead of a pity party, Paul and Silas had a Holy Ghost party, as they prayed and sang hymns of praise to the Almighty.

Praise accomplishes wonders.

The anointing was so strong, the other prisoners and the guard could not help but listen in amazement. Heaven took note of this pure and precious praise and responded as God rocked the place in delight. The foundations of the prison were shaken, and every man's shackles were broken; they were free. That's the thing about praise!

Benjamin William Hastings sings it best in a song entitled "That's the Thing About Praise." I urge to you listen to it when you have the chance. Praise despite your mountain, your walls or your chains, and watch the Almighty work. That's the thing about praise! Hallelujah! Hallelujah!!!
PENNY DIS

PENNY DIS

Takeaway(s) / New Idea(s)

_____

_____

_____

_____

_____

Commitment(s)

_____

_____

_____

_____

_____

Prayer / Thanksgiving / Resolution(s)

_____

_____

_____

_____

_____

33

WHAT HAVE YOU GOT IN YOUR HAND?

The chorus of a gospel song by Alvin Slaughter comes to mind which asks, "what you have got in your hand?" The Lord, EL SHADDAI, will supply more than you need if you will just use the little that you've got.

After Moses made a fool of himself when he tried to liberate the children of Israel from their Egyptian slavery, he ran away to Midian and spent forty years in "God's classroom" in the backside of the desert tending his father-in-law's herds. (God has a way of taking His errant children to school, His school of wisdom.)

When he had learned his lesson in humility, God now called and commissioned Moses to the same task that he previously failed, but this time, he was under new management: God Himself. The, once impulsive, Moses now said he can't, which was partly truth and partly falsehood. He couldn't, in *his own* strength, but could by God's almighty power. After myriads of excuses, which seemed to try God's patience, God asked Moses, "What have you got in your hand?" Moses' response was 'just a staff (stick).' God told Moses to cast it on the ground and Moses complied. The stick was transformed into a venomous snake.

Moses was then told by God to do something that we might think ridiculously foolish and also dangerous. He was told to take the snake by its tail. *Are you kidding me? The snake will surely bite me with deadly consequences!* Moses obeyed though, and the serpent transformed back into the original stick. With other miracles, God eventually convinced Moses to follow orders and deliver God's people. With a stick, Moses plagued Egypt and even parted the Red Sea. A mere stick under God's anointing can work Marvelous wonders.

A little boy set out one day to hear Jesus preaching about the kingdom of God. His wise mother fixed a boy-sized lunch of five barley loaves and two small fish. She had figured he would be out past lunchtime and had planned for his refreshment. Wise woman indeed!

As it turned out, Jesus preached past the noon hour and well into the early afternoon. The disciples pleaded with Jesus to cut the message short and to send the crowd away to seek food for they must have been hungry. Jesus told the disciples to do the "ridiculous" (God just loves to test our faith). He told them to feed the people. The little boy perceived the dilemma and magnanimously offered up the lunch that was in his hands. A disciple, when asked by Jesus what they had?" they said that they had only five loaves and two small fish, but added, 'What is this for the need of so many?' Jesus did the rest. He had the disciples seat the crowd into manageable groups. Then He asked His heavenly Father to sanctify and multiply the puny meal, and the disciples distributed it to the multitude: over five thousand men, besides women and children had a belly full and twelve baskets of fragments were collected as leftovers.

With a stick, Moses plagued Egypt and even parted the Red Sea.

For David, it was a sling. God used David's mastery of his slingshot to slay the giant Goliath. For Dorcas, it was a knitting needle. God used her craft to clothe and warm countless needy women. What do you have in your hand? God can use it, if you're willing to believe it and do what The Lord compels you to do with it.

The song "That's When" by Alvin Slaughter reminds that God can take what you have and make it grand. So, what have you got in your hand? Or better yet, what has God given you? If you will consecrate it to the Master and prayerfully stay in the moment, wonderful eternal things will be done through it. So, what you have got in your hands may seem insignificant to men and even to you, but that is when it is *your* in hands. Give it to God in absolute surrender and watch what God will do

with it. A waiting world depends on your obedience.
PENNY DIS

PENNY DIS

Takeaway(s) / New Idea(s)

_____

_____

_____

_____

_____

Commitment(s)

_____

_____

_____

_____

_____

Prayer / Thanksgiving / Resolution(s)

_____

_____

_____

_____

_____

34

MADE FOR MORE

You know the story, don't you, about a misfit duckling who later found out why he didn't fit in with the rest of his so-called siblings? One day, a flock of white swans flew overhead, and something resonated in his heart. He suddenly found where he belonged as he joined them in graceful flight. He was not an ugly duckling but a beautiful and graceful swan. Have I gotten the attention of a misfit? Maybe you aren't who you think you are. Maybe, just maybe, you were made for something more.

Nature (God's handiwork) has so many lessons to teach us. That creepy-crawly dirt-bound caterpillar can be so repulsive (at least to many of the female sex). As boys, we found them fascinating. There comes a time in spring when these crawlers attach themselves to a stem or leaf, spin a cocoon about themselves, and a wonderful transformation begins (metamorphosis) from the inside out. What later emerges are beautiful sky-bound, nectar-eating butterflies. These, too, come to recognize that they were made for something more as they fill the skies with their wonder and majesty.

Esther was a Jewish girl of humble descent, orphaned at a tender age and raised by her elder cousin named Mordecai. Through an amazing and God-orchestrated series of events, Esther rose from obscurity to become the queen of the Persian Empire. She would save her Jewish people, as she was challenged by her guardian Mordecai with the question, 'Who is to tell whether you were brought to the throne (by God) for such a time as this?' Esther was the agent through which Divine Providence was extended to her nation.

Mary, the mother of our Saviour Jesus Christ, was a humble, godly virgin who was visited by the messenger angel Gabriel.

'Hail, thou who art highly favoured (by God), blessed art thou amongst women. The Holy Ghost will come upon you and the power of the Most High will overshadow you. You will conceive and bear a Son, who you will call Jesus, for He shall save His people from their sins.'

The miracle of the immaculate conception took place in this pure, sweet maiden.

Joseph was the penultimate son of Jacob, the first son of Jacob by his favoured wife, Rachel. Joseph was given the menial, but very important, task of tending his father's sheep. This was a smelly, meticulous and, often, dangerous occupation, for at times, Joseph had to protect the vulnerable animals from ferocious predators. But God had something more in store for this young man who was his father's favourite. However, because he was his father's favourite, Joseph was despised by his older brothers. He was sold into slavery. Through divine detours: slavery to Potiphar; imprisonment for his fidelity to his God; and being delivered and elevated to the second most powerful man in Egypt, by which means he fulfilled his divine destiny of saving his family as God had revealed to him, you can see that Joseph truly was made for more.

Those who have completely submitted their lives to Jesus Christ
find that little becomes much when placed in the Master's hands,
and their lives become so much more.

Another shepherd boy rose from obscurity to become Israel's greatest historical king. You know of whom I speak, the sweet Psalmist and great king David. David started off in early life being just a shepherd, but when others only saw him just as such, God saw in him a man after His own heart who was fit for Israel's throne. He slew the giant to deliver Israel from the Philistines, became the most successful leader of Israel's army, was envied and savagely hunted to be murdered by king Saul, but many years later fulfilled his divine destiny to become one of the greatest kings the world has ever known.

Maybe your life seems ordinary and insignificant to you right now, but those who have completely submitted their lives to Jesus Christ find that little becomes much when placed in the Master's hands, and their lives become so much more. If you haven't already done so, submit your life to Jesus right now, and you too will find that you were made for something more.
PENNY DIS

PENNY DIS

Takeaway(s) / New Idea(s)

_____

_____

_____

_____

_____

Commitment(s)

_____

_____

_____

_____

_____

Prayer / Thanksgiving / Resolution(s)

_____

_____

_____

_____

_____

35

NOT IN CLOSETS

Funeral services give opportunity to put away the remains of the dead in a dignified manner. "Ashes to ashes, dust to dust" is the signal to lower the casket, six-foot-six (with the price of land, I don't think they are so generous anymore), and to seal and cover the dead. People with common sense know that skeletons belong in cemeteries, so why do so many people keep them in their closets?

I suppose the trend started with Adam and Eve. They sinned against God and proceeded to hide among the trees in Eden, covering their nakedness with fig leaves. Where can we possibly hide from the Almighty?

'Where can I go (to get away from) Your Spirit? Where can I flee from Your presence? If I go up to the heavens, You are there. If I make my bed in hell, behold You are there. If I take the wings of the dawn, and dwell in the uttermost part of the sea, even there, Your hand will guide me; Your right hand will hold me fast' (Psalm 139:7–10).

'Adam, where are you?' (Genesis 3:9). A rhetorical question. God knew exactly where Adam was and what he had done. It was time to take the skeleton out of the closet.

Cain followed in his father Adam's footsteps. "Where is your brother?" (Genesis 4:9, NLT) Another of God's rhetorical questions. God was there when He murdered Abel. Once again, it was time to get the skeleton out of the closet. Cain paid a monumental price for his murderous deed.

Achan was tempted by the wedge of gold, the two hundred shekels of silver and the Babylonian garment, and he yielded. Joshua 7:1 referred to his deed as "committing the accursed thing." All the plunder belonged to God. 'Keep away from the devoted things, so that you will not bring about your own destruction by taking any of them.' *But who could possibly know if I indulge myself secretly?*" Achan surely thought. Achan, "The eyes of the LORD are in every place, beholding the evil and the good" (Proverbs 15:3, KJV). When, as a result, Israel was soundly and embarrassingly defeated by Ai (little both in length of name and size), Joshua was commanded by God to find the culprit, and to punish him. Things were beginning to show themselves. Achan had every opportunity to "fess up" and take the skeleton out of the closet, but he was hoping he could get away with it. Did he not remember that God is the revealer of secret things?

Israel came forward to Joshua by tribes, and the tribe of Judah was taken. Judah came forward by clans. The Zerahites were taken. The noose tightened. The Zerahites came forward by families. Zimri was taken. Achan's judgment was imminent. Zimri's family came forward, man by man. Time is up Achan! Achan, the son of Zimri, the son of Zerah, of the tribe of Judah was taken.

Achan was made to publicly declare the evil that he had committed. (Something similar will happen in the final judgment in Revelation). His entire family was stoned to death to remove the blight on Israel. What a calamity!

The sweet Psalmist, also Israel's greatest historical king (David), similarly tried unsuccessfully to hide his skeletons in a closet. He committed adultery with Bathsheba (Uriah's wife who became pregnant) and conspired to commit murder when his plan to get Uriah to sleep with his wife failed. He wanted to give Uriah a "well-tailored suit" (sometimes called a jacket) after the resulting pregnancy. (How many times has it happened that one act of sexual indiscretion has resulted in pregnancy?) With Uriah dead, David married Bathsheba and presumed that no one was counting months, so the baby on the way would be considered conceived in wedlock.

Everything was "copasetic." *This will be our little secret Bathsheba*, or so David thought. How many know that God loves us too much to leave us in unconfessed sin? You know the story. The prophet Nathan told David a wise story.

David passed judgment on the story's villain. Nathan declared to David, "thou art the man" (2 Samuel 12:7). It was time for David to take the skeletons out of his closet. David humbly acknowledged and confessed his sin. God graciously forgave him, but the consequences of his transgressions were grave. There is always a *high* price for *low* living.

People with common sense know

that skeletons belong in cemeteries,

so why do so many people

keep them in their closets?

The baby died. David's son raped his half-sister. Her brother avenged her by murdering her rapist. David's beloved and rottenly spoilt son overthrew his father, he slept with his father's concubines in the view of all Israel, and David's life ended in great sorrow. Who is to tell that had David volunteered his confession earlier, he could have spared himself all of this heartache?

Coming closer to the present, Ananias and Sapphira learnt the hard way that skeletons don't belong in closets. They coveted the honour given those who sold land and gave all the proceeds to the apostles to meet the needs of the poor and destitute Christians. They, too, sold land but kept back part of the proceeds (which was their right to do), but they publicly declared that they gave it all. They basked in the glorious accolades given by the church, but that didn't last long. The Spirit revealed their sin of deception to the apostle Peter. Peter met Ananias privately (without his wife's knowledge) and inquired, 'Did you sell your land for such and such an amount?'

'Oh yes, Pastor Peter. We sold the land for that amount and gave all the proceeds to the church.'

'How is it (Ananias) that Satan has filled your heart to attempt to deceive the Holy Spirit? You have not lied to men, but to God' (Acts 5:3–4). At these words, Ananias fell dead at the apostle's feet and was taken out and buried. Three hours later, Mrs. Ananias came to Peter, oblivious to what had transpired with her expired husband. The same question was asked. 'Did you sell your land for such and such amount?' Same response:

'Oh yes, Pastor Peter. We sold the land for that amount and gave all the proceeds to the church.'

Peter replied, "How is it that ye have agreed together to tempt the Spirit of the Lord? behold, the feet of them which have buried thy husband are at the door, and shall carry thee out "(Acts 5:9, KJV). At these words Sapphira fell dead and was taken and buried (I suppose lying beside her lying husband).

"If we confess our sins, he is faithful and just to forgive us our sins, and to cleanse us from all unrighteousness" (1 John 1:9, KJV). Brothers and sisters, let us not trifle with God. If you or I have skeletons in our closets, it is just a matter of time before HE reveals it. Isn't it better that we voluntarily confess it and face the consequences? Aren't you suffering enough by the condemnation of your guilty conscience? Read what happened to David in Psalm 32 when he tried to "cover up." It is far better to cast ourselves at the mercy of God than to face the wrath of God. Yes, there may be a price to pay, but our penalty will be far less severe.

So, let us bring those decayed bones out of the closet and out in the open for burial. Let us confess to God (and possibly to men) what we have done (and have been doing), receive HIS forgiveness and face the consequences. We too, like David, will enjoy the blessing of he whose transgression is forgiven, whose sin is covered by the grace of God.

PENNY DIS

Takeaway(s) / New Idea(s)

___

___

___

___

___

Commitment(s)

___

___

___

___

___

Prayer / Thanksgiving / Resolution(s)

___

___

___

___

___

PENNY DIS

36

WHAT'S IN A NAME?

What's in a name? For the most part, nothing really. I believe a literary scholar once said, "A rose by any other name would be just as sweet." Some personal names seem to predestine people for greatness: Englebert Humperdinck or Wolf Blitzer, for example. With names like these, you will certainly stand out. A person's name can be a source of great pride or of exceeding embarrassment.

In the course of teaching, I have met international students with peculiar (but quite delightful) names, such as "Blessing," "Rainbow" and "Monday." When it comes to Bible names, I sometimes wonder if the meaning of a certain name preceded the person or if the person's character defined the name. For example, "Nabal" means "fool" and he was true to his name. Jezebel has come to define a woman of evil character. Judas has come to mean betrayer.

The name for God's Son was not haphazardly chosen. As we have seen from the scriptures, the Virgin Mary was told by the angel Gabriel, 'And you shall bring forth a son, and you shall call His name JESUS, for HE shall save HIS people from their sins.' "JESUS," like "YESHUA," means JEHOVAH saves, and is linked to His divine role as Messiah. Jesus Christ is God, veiled in human flesh. 'In the beginning was the Word, and the Word was with God, and the Word was God. The same was in the beginning with God... and the Word took on flesh and dwelt amongst us...' (Saint John 1:2; 1:14).

The name of Jesus is an all-powerful one. On the day of Pentecost, Peter boldly declared, "Therefore let all Israel (and all people) be assured of this: God has made this Jesus, whom you crucified, both Lord and Christ."

"SALVATION" is in the name of Jesus (and Jesus alone). Peter declared to the Sanhedrin, "Neither is there salvation in any other: for there is none other name under heaven given among men, whereby we must be saved" (Acts 4:12, KJV).

"HEALING" is in the name of Jesus. Peter told the lame man outside the Beautiful Gate, 'Silver and gold have I none, but such that I have I give to you. In the name of Jesus Christ of Nazareth, stand and walk' (Acts 3:6). The man not only rose to his feet and walked, but he also leapt for joy.

"DELIVERANCE" is in the name of Jesus. Just as we read before, the Apostle Paul met a slave girl who was possessed by an evil spirit of divination. As we have read, Paul was so burdened by her bondage that he said to the spirit in her, " In the name of Jesus Christ, I command you to come out of her." At that very moment, that spirit left her; she was delivered.

What a beautiful name it is, a wonderful name it is, a powerful name it is, the name of Jesus. Satan and his demonic hosts tremble at the name of Jesus. The elements and all nature obey

His voice. The dead respond to His command. Jesus said that on a future day that hose in the grave will hear His voice and be resurrected, either to eternal life or eternal damnation, 'Wherefore God has also highly exalted Him (Jesus) and given Him a name above all other, that at the name of Jesus, every knee shall bow, and every tongue confess that Jesus is Lord, to The glory of God the Father' (Philippians 2:9).

The name for God's Son was not haphazardly chosen.

Jesus Christ, my friend, will either be your Saviour or your divine Judge, and this judge comes not as gentle Jesus, but as the Lion of the tribe of Judah, to execute tribulation and wrath on those who rejected Him and His salvation. You most certainly will not want to stand before His Great White throne on that fateful day.

Brothers and sisters, don't be afraid to speak His name (Jesus), to praise His name, to cast down principalities and powers in His name. What's in a name? If

it is the name of *Jesus*, there is everything wonderful in it. Say the name, even when in grief and pain.
JESUS!!!
Hallelujah!
PENNY DIS

PENNY DIS

Takeaway(s) / New Idea(s)

___

___

___

___

___

Commitment(s)

___

___

___

___

___

Prayer / Thanksgiving / Resolution(s)

___

___

___

___

___

37

THE ULTIMATE TRANSFORMATION

An eminent sculptor was asked the secret to his long and successful career. "How do you transform cold slabs of marble into wonderful works of art? He thoughtfully replied, "I have an image in my mind, and I systematically remove from the slab everything that does not conform to that image." An amazing response!

It got me thinking about the ultimate transformation: God systematically changing the redeemed sinner into the image of His Son Jesus Christ. This is a process that can take many decades to complete.

Salvation. "Believe on the Lord Jesus Christ, and thou shalt be saved" (Acts 16:31, KJV)

Sanctification. " Present yourselves to God as being alive from the dead, and your members as instruments of righteousness to God" (Romans 6:13, NKJV). This means putting away sin.

Transformation. 'But we all, with unveiled face, beholding as in a mirror the Glory of the Lord (Jesus), are being transformed into the same image, from glory to glory, just as by the Spirit of the Lord' 2 Corinthians 3:18.

Glorification (The impartation of a "Holy Spirit glow"). 'That Moses did not know that the skin of his face shone while he talked with Him (God). So, when Aaron and all the children of Israel saw Moses, behold the skin of his face shone...' (Exodus 34:29–30).

Consummation. Permanent and irreversible Christlikeness. 'Beloved, now are we the sons of God and it has not yet been revealed what we shall be, but we know that when He is revealed (at the rapture) we shall be like Him, for we shall see Him as He is' (1 John 3:2).

This process of transformation is catalyzed by tribulations. '(Paul) strengthening the disciples, exhorted them to continue in the faith, saying: We must go through many tribulations to enter the kingdom of God' (Acts 14:22). Romans 5:3 says we must press on 'knowing this, that tribulation worketh patience, and patience experience, and experience hope...' 'That the trial of your faith, being much more precious than gold that perisheth, though it is tested by fire, may be found to be worthy of praise, honour and glory at the revelation of Jesus Christ' (1 Peter 1:7).

This process of transformation is catalyzed by tribulations.

As the master sculptor uses sledgehammer, saw, grate, sander, chisel and knife to remove everything that does not conform to the image in view, in like manner God uses a variety of trials and tribulations to ultimately change the redeemed sinner, saved by sovereign Grace, into the perfect image of His Son Jesus Christ.

So, my brothers and sisters, that impossible boss, that disturbing neighbour, that ungrateful congregation, that "thorn in the flesh" (referred to in 2 Corinthians 12:7) serves a divine purpose, "Christlikeness." Instead of complaining, we should be rejoicing as Christ is working in us, so He can work through us.

I close with a reflection from some of the words of a song from Sunday School, "He's Still Working on Me," sung by the Hemphills. It took God just a week to make the moon and the stars. How loving and patient He must be to still be working on me.

PENNY DIS

Takeaway(s) / New Idea(s)

_____
_____
_____
_____
_____

Commitment(s)

_____
_____
_____
_____
_____

Prayer / Thanksgiving / Resolution(s)

_____
_____
_____
_____
_____

PENNY DIS

38

THE POWER OF ONE

Whether it was at Rose Preparatory School or at Harbour View Primary, I am not quite certain, but as a child I learned a memory "gem":

For Want of a Nail
For want of a nail, a shoe was lost.
For want of a shoe, a horse was lost.
For want of a horse, a soldier was lost.
For want of a soldier, a detail was lost.
For want of a detail, a battle was lost.
For want of a battle, the war was lost.

Who could have thought that victory or defeat in a great war, would rest in the fate of a single nail?

It got me thinking about the power of one, for good or for evil. How many times have you and I downplayed the significance of one: just one lie, just one stolen sweet, just one illicit sexual act, just one abortion? What's the big deal? Did you ever stop to think that one act of disobedience in the Garden of Eden plunged the entire human race into sin? Have you ever contemplated that one act of indiscrete anger caused Moses not to enter the Promised Land? Only one lie resulted in the instant death of Ananias and Sapphira? Many times, one is one too many.

On the other hand, do you realize that one act of obedience by the prophet Jonah (though he was reluctant) led to the salvation of the great city of Nineveh? Or that the widow's mite (or two) was more valuable to Jesus than all the money of the wealth poured into the treasury on that fateful day? Or ponder how the faithfulness of Daniel resulted in a pagan king mandating his entire realm to worship the true and living God? Or better yet, how the blood shed by the sinless Son of God makes it possible for sinners like you and me to have forgiveness and peace with a thrice holy God? Never, ever underestimate the power of one.

One act of obedience by the prophet Jonah (though he was reluctant) led to the salvation of the great city of Nineveh.

Another of the saddest verses in the Bible is found in Ezekiel 22:30. The Lord says, "And I sought for a man among them, that should make up the hedge, and stand in the gap before me for the land, that I should not destroy it: but I found none" (KJV). What an indictment! Thank God, there is redemption; as the triune God still asks today as He did in Isaiah's day, "Whom shall We send, and who will go for us?" May we join Isaiah in saying, "Lord, here am I, send me."

PENNY DIS

Takeaway(s) / New Idea(s)

_____

_____

_____

_____

_____

Commitment(s)

_____

_____

_____

_____

_____

Prayer / Thanksgiving / Resolution(s)

_____

_____

_____

_____

_____

39

TOO BUSY DOING WHAT?

You may well have heard the story of a pious lady, who dreamt one night that Jesus would visit her the following day. At the crack of dawn, she set about putting her house in order and preparing a sumptuous meal for her "Visitor from heaven."

As she busied herself, her doorbell rang. There stood a dishevelled and ragged vagrant. She had no time for such distraction, so she curtly dismissed him and sent him away. She furtively continued with her preparations.

Later that afternoon, the doorbell rang again, this time it was a very young mother with her needy baby. A second time, this churched woman dismissed the intruders as she had "bigger fish to fry."

The rest of the day passed without her "VIP" arriving. The woman went to bed that night disappointed and disillusioned. God came to her in a dream, saying how disappointed He was, coming twice to her house and being turned away each time. The woman was puzzled. "When did I see You and turned You away?" she asked.

"I visited you in the person of that hungry vagrant and that needy young mother," He replied. She was "too busy" but doing what?

Jesus told a story we call "The Parable of the Good Samaritan" in Saint Luke's Gospel, in answer to a question, "And who is my neighbour?" A Jewish man, traveling from Jerusalem to Jericho, was set upon by thieves who beat and robbed him and left him to die. Two deeply religious Jewish men (a priest and a Levite. happened to come upon their wounded countryman, but they had their religious duties to perform and were far too busy doing "God's work" to stop and help this man. However, a Samaritan came by (a stranger and sworn enemy), attended to the battered man's wounds, made accommodation for his lodging at an inn, and pledged to pay any outstanding costs on a future return. Like the priest and the Levite, we can be too busy, but busy doing what?

I am amazed by Philip the Evangelist. He was leading a revival in Samaria. He was preaching. The Spirit was moving. People were being saved and baptized in droves. Heaven had come down to Earth. In the middle of great success, the Spirit bade Philip to take the desert road leading to seemingly nowhere. Without questioning, Philip obeyed and as a result, led the Ethiopian eunuch to Christ and in the process initiated the Gospel's entry into Africa through a man he met only once (and who could have been considered a distraction).

Like the priest and the Levite, we can be too busy, but busy doing what?

Again, I ask, too busy doing what? What is God's work? Is it not reaching the lost with the gospel? When our daily plans and activities are "disrupted" by people in need, be reminded, God might just be paying us a visit.

Takeaway(s) / New Idea(s)

_____

_____

_____

_____

_____

Commitment(s)

_____

_____

_____

_____

_____

Prayer / Thanksgiving / Resolution(s)

_____

_____

_____

_____

_____

PENNY DIS

40

WHAT (OR WHOM) ARE YOU WILLING TO DIE FOR?

A passionate beau who wanted to impress his belle told her, "For you, I would swim the deepest ocean. For you, I would climb the highest mountain. For you, my darling, I would cross the most severe desert." As they were parting, she inquired when next she would see him. His response... "Tomorrow, if it does not rain."

Words are so cheap. Actions are much more eloquent. But actions must be of one's volition. I heard, once, of a king who had one precious daughter. He wanted to ensure that the man who married her was deserving of his priceless jewel. He set up a one-mile-long pool and filled it with ferocious crocodiles, and offered her hand in marriage to any man who would survive the one-mile ordeal. The bravest of men in the realm came, but none dared to risk his life, not even to wed her. Suddenly, there was a splash, and a man swam desperately for his life, with crocs in tow. He miraculously survived the perilous course. The king was ecstatic. "You are a worthy son-in-law. You must love my daughter."

"Love your daughter?!" he exclaimed incredibly. I *waan* ketch the joker who pitched me in!" Is there anyone you would give your life for?

Words are so cheap.

Actions are much more eloquent.

One ex-president's lawyer once said he would take a bullet for his client. He later gave evidence to impeach the ex-President. Words are so cheap!

After a ferocious fire that completely destroyed his farm, a farmer went to survey the damage after it subsided. It was total devastation. In disgust, he kicked one of the charred remains, and, to his complete surprise, six chicks ran away in fright. The charred remains were that of the chicks' mother which had sheltered them from the fiery furnace.

There is One who gave His life for you and for me. I remember vividly singing ignorantly about Him at Daily Vacation Bible School in the early 1970s as a preteen, led passionately by Missionary Frank Fenton at Harbour View Gospel Chapel. I sang about how He suffered and died for me. Back then, Saint John 3:16 was just a verse to memorize for a prize, but now *He* means everything to me. "For God so loved the world, that he gave his only begotten Son, that whosoever believeth in him should not perish, but have everlasting life." Jesus said in Saint John 15:13, " Greater love has no one than this, than to lay down one's life for his friends" (NKJV). Romans 5:7–9 says, 'Scarcely for a righteous man would one die; yet peradventure, for a good man, some may even dare to die. But God commended His love to us, that while we were yet sinners (yet sinning), Christ died for us.'

PENNY DIS

Have you embraced this loving Saviour and received His unconditional love? If so, don't keep such wonderful news to yourself. Tell it and tell it every opportunity you get. If not, then heed the words of Psalm 2:12 which say, "Kiss the Son, lest he be angry, and ye perish *from* the way"(KJV)—the way to eternal life and to making Jesus happy in you. PENNY DIS.

Takeaway(s) / New Idea(s)

_____

_____

_____

_____

_____

Commitment(s)

_____

_____

_____

_____

_____

Prayer / Thanksgiving / Resolution(s)

_____

_____

_____

_____

_____

About the Author

Robert (Bobby J) Jackson is a Christian and career teacher of Mathematics for over forty years. A proud Jamaican who migrated to Canada in 2007, he is the husband of one wife, Sandra Marie, since 1989. Though not a biological father, he has been a father figure to many children and young people over the years. His love for God, and sharp sense of humour, have endeared him to the Christian community at home and abroad. He enjoys gardening and landscaping. Robert and Sandra are members of Hope Church Mississauga in Ontario Canada.

Image Credits:

Adirondack chairs in a serene setting by mynewturtle at 123RF.com, front cover

www.ingramcontent.com/pod-product-compliance
Lightning Source LLC
Chambersburg PA
CBHW071307110426
42743CB00042B/1200